HGTV

CURB APPEAL

Meredith® Books
Des Moines, Iowa

HGTV Curb Appeal

Editor: Paula Marshall
Contributing Writer: Melissa Bigner
Contributing Editors: Catherine Staub, Julie Collins—Lexicon Consulting
Contributing Designer: David Jordan—Studio 22
Copy Chief: Terri Fredrickson
Publishing Operations Manager: Karen Schirm
Senior Editor, Asset and Information Manager: Phillip Morgan
Edit and Design Production Coordinator: Mary Lee Gavin
Editorial Assistant: Kaye Chabot
Book Production Managers: Pam Kvitne, Marjorie J. Schenkelberg, Rick von Holdt, Mark Weaver
Contributing Copy Editor: Ira Lacher
Contributing Proofreaders: Dan Degen, Cindy Lewis, Ann Marie Sapienza
Contributing Photographer: Jamie Hadley
Indexer: Kathleen Poole

Meredith® Books
Executive Director, Editorial: Gregory H. Kayko
Executive Director, Design: Matt Strelecki
Managing Editor: Amy Tincher-Durik
Executive Editor/Group Manager: Denise Caringer
Associate Design Director: Chad Jewell
Marketing Product Manager: Tyler Woods

Publisher and Editor in Chief: James D. Blume
Editorial Director: Linda Raglan Cunningham
Executive Director, New Business Development: Todd M. Davis
Executive Director, Sales: Ken Zagor
Director, Operations: George A. Susral
Director, Production: Douglas M. Johnston
Director, Marketing: Amy Nichols
Business Director: Jim Leonard
Vice President and General Manager: Douglas J. Guendel

Meredith Publishing Group
President: Jack Griffin
Executive Vice President: Bob Mate

Meredith Corporation
Chairman and Chief Executive Officer: William T. Kerr
President and Chief Operating Officer: Stephen M. Lacy
In Memoriam: E.T. Meredith III (1933-2003)

All of us at Meredith® Books are dedicated to providing you with information and ideas to enhance your home. We welcome your comments and suggestions. Write to us at: Meredith Books, Home Decorating and Design Editorial Department, 1716 Locust St., Des Moines, IA 50309-3023.

All materials provided in this book by or on behalf of HGTV or otherwise associated with HGTV's program *Curb Appeal* and owned by Scripps Networks, Inc. are used under license by Meredith Corporation. "HGTV," "Home & Garden Television," the HGTV logo, and the title "Curb Appeal" are service marks and/or trademarks of Scripps Networks, Inc.

Curb Appeal is produced by Edelman Productions.

HGTV CURB APPEAL

A stroll through any neighborhood tells the tale:

Some houses have "it" and some don't. The "it" is curb appeal—that special something that makes you do a double take when you spot a gem of a house. Houses with curb appeal seem to sit perfectly on the land, express the architectural AND the homeowner's styles, and exude a sense of welcoming. If you've always dreamed of living in such a place—with a luscious lawn and perfect paint job to boot—don't pack your bags and go house hunting. More than likely you're living in a diamond in the rough. And now the experts at HGTV's hit show *Curb Appeal* are here to help you polish it with panache.

With loads of advice, tips, and doable ideas direct from the show, this book provides you with a path to realizing your house makeover dreams. Novices and pro do-it-yourselfers will find major and minor landscaping and home exterior projects that they can pull off in a weekend or less—without breaking the bank. And those who don't like to get their hands dirty will revel in the inspiring photos of *Curb Appeal* favorites and the detailed instructions for creating rock-solid contracts and hiring the best crews around. Whichever camp you fall into, head streetside with this workbook-slash-lookbook, because that's where reality starts—and where *Curb Appeal* dreams come true.

Chapters

1 2 3 4 5

1 GET STARTED

Curb appeal is all about good first impressions and lasting good impressions. Here's how to evaluate the elements of curb appeal on your home and begin your home-front transformation.

2 DRESS UP THE HOUSE

From the curb, it's character—great entry, nicely dressed windows, and a tip-top roof—that invites homeowners in at the end of the day, and welcomes guests as they walk up to the door. Find out how to improve these key elements of your home.

3 COLOR YOUR WORLD

Tune into this insider know-how to determine your dream color scheme, learn what colors to paint where, and discover tips on how to wield a paintbrush (and roller—let's be practical here!) like a pro.

4 WELCOME HOME

In a perfect world, pulling into your driveway or walking the path from the street to your front door should inspire you and give you a serene feeling every day. Here'show to step up the paths (and drives) to your front door.

5 FRAME YOUR YARD

It's time to play border patrol and determine what fences, walls, hedges, gates, and such you'll employ to best frame your landscape-to-be. Learn how defining your space can be as simple as digging holes for a hedge or stacking stones for a short wall.

6 7 8 9

ROOM TO RELAX

There's no finer way to soak in the great outdoors than by sitting in the middle of it. Bring the comforts of indoor living outdoors, so you can best enjoy the benefits of your *Curb Appeal* project.

MASTER LANDSCAPING

Leave it to Mother Nature to soften the edges of the most austere architecture and make the sweetest cottage more endearing. As seen from the curb, a dream combo of trees, shrubs, flowerbeds, and groundcovers flow out from any front door like a red-carpet welcome. Give your address that same open-arm feeling.

FINISH WITH DETAILS

How does a home polish off its look? With address markers, mailboxes, water fountains, outdoor lanterns, and more—all finishing details that make a house either fashionably of-the-moment, a timeless classic, or a funky standout. Follow these expressive ideas for making your home a standout success.

DO THE HOMEWORK

Curb Appeal episodes seem to come off without a hitch. What you don't see are run-ins with local neighborhood associations, sites shutting down thanks to code violations, or area evacuations due to gas leaks. Here's the backstory on making your curb-appeal redo operate as smoothly as the show.

1

GET STARTED

Put Your Best Face Forward

Curb appeal is all about good first impressions and lasting good impressions, the friendly sense of invitation that a well-designed home exterior projects to homeowners, to guests, and to passersby. If you're not entirely satisfied with the street side of your house, you've come to the right place.

Before you dive into fix-it mode, however, take a moment to give your homestead an honest curbside analysis. Diagnose what's working and what's not to create a plan for your home front revival. You'll save yourself both headaches and cash in large measure if you start with an honest self-appraisal. Learn how to walk through the assessment process the *Curb Appeal* experts employ, find advice to get your home improvement imagination jump started, and create a plan for setting your home exterior makeover adventure in motion, one can-do project at a time.

Give Your House the Once-Over

Walk out to the curb and look at your house. Pretend you're seeing it for the first time. Even though it's your home, be tough, really tough. Scrutinize the front of your home as thoroughly as a dad checking out his daughter's first date!

On the first pass focus specifically on the structures of the house and garage. Think about these points:

> **The front door.** Every home should have a focal

point. When you look at something large, such as the front of a house, your eye needs a place to start taking it all in. If your house doesn't have one, no matter what you do to fix it up, it will always feel unfinished. The best choice for an exterior focal point is the front door. It's the one thing everyone should be able to find—especially first-time guests. If yours is covered by landscaping or hidden under the eaves, make a note of the problem.

> **The path.** Once the door is prominent, the way to get there should be unimpeded. Overgrown bushes, sharp turns, and a narrow clearance are a few things that make the trip to your front door difficult.

> **The house numbers.** On *Curb Appeal*, you may notice the house numbers are often redone. That's because if you can't see them from the street, or they're not where you expect to see them, they're pointless.

Night Eyes

Go back and look at your house at night. In this viewing, focus on security.
• Is your front door lit in a safe and an inviting manner?
• Is the path to the door—from the street and from the garage—clear, well-lit, and safe?
• Can you see the house number clearly from the street?

LEFT: Now this is curb appeal! A clearly defined path and entry work with a well-planned landscape to enliven a small lot. Good curb appeal doesn't have to involve lavish plants and extravagant features.

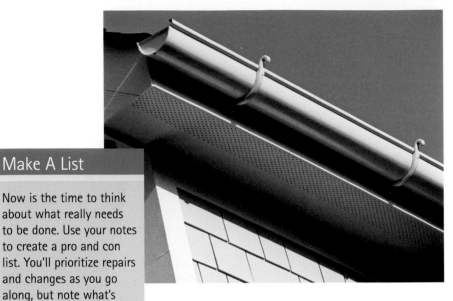

Make A List

Now is the time to think about what really needs to be done. Use your notes to create a pro and con list. You'll prioritize repairs and changes as you go along, but note what's really in bad shape or what really bugs you.

> **The mailbox.** If a new mail-delivery person has to play hide-and-seek to find the mailbox, put it on your list of things to improve. After all you want to know if Ed McMahon has a special delivery for you!

> **The details.** At this point big-ticket items and quick fixes are all lumped together. Sorting and prioritizing comes later. So look at your home's add-ons, such as light fixtures, shutters, columns, and railings. Check out

the trim work around the windows and doors. If your house has overhangs, porticoes, awnings, or a porch, be sure to evaluate them as well. Do these things fit with your house? Are they the right size and scale, and in the right style to make sense with your home's architecture? Note what you'd like to change.

> **The working elements.** Look at things such as gutters, siding, shutters, and the like. Are they in good condition, or do they practically cry out for repairs?

> **The color.** While this is often the first thing you see, it may not be the first thing you should change. Think of color as part of the whole package. Does the color scheme welcome, soothe, and inspire you as you pull up to the house? If not, put it on the list.

> **The garage (or carport).** Give this structure the same thorough going-over that you gave the house. Is it connected to the house, not only physically but also stylistically?

> **The clean factor.** Even if you have all the details pulled together, upkeep makes the package. Note whether your house looks fresh, clean, and well-kept.

Don't You Dare Skip Repairs

Before you skip out to play, you have to do your chores. In the home makeover world, that means tending to repair work first, before diving into the fun and games of color and landscaping. Act like a house inspector and ask these questions:

Does the house suffer from rot, holes, or major cracks?

What condition is the siding in?

Do doors, windows, and gates open and close easily?

Are all railings sound, or do they jiggle?

Are there missing elements (shutters or rail spindles, for example)?

Are steps and paths even and safe to walk upon?

Is the drive cracked and uneven?

Do lighting and electrical systems function?

ABOVE: Examine your home's siding, trim, and gutters to ensure they look good and function well.

OPPOSITE: Take a step back and scrutinize every detail of your house. The right mix of supporting elements, including shutters, columns, and railings, are pivotal for creating true curb appeal.

Get the Lay of the Land

Turn that same discerning eye to focus specifically on the landscape (living things such as plants, trees, and groundcovers), and the hardscape (inanimate objects such as walkways, structures, and retention walls)—essentially everything aside from the house and garage.

As before, focus first on entering the home and consider these points:

> **A place to park.** You pull in the drive every day, but is it clear where guests should park?

> **A path to the door.** When you looked at the house, the entryway was scrutinized; now's the time to look at the route a visitor would take from the street to the door. Is it obvious, inviting, and safe?

> **Yard details.** If you have yard structures such as gates, fences, arbors, and pergolas, do they make sense where they are? Is your yard empty and begging for such embellishments?

> **The plants.** Do the plants complement the house and set a mood that appeals to you? If the gardens were simply there when you moved in and you've been doing maintenance since, take the time now to consider what you want in a garden—including size, amount of care required, and location.

> **The trees.** Do the trees accent the home, or do they hide it? Trees are a tough one: They're a bonus to any home, but the wrong tree in the wrong place can be a maintenance nightmare. At this point, consider only the pros and cons of the trees you have.

> **The lawn.** Do you have a lawn or a barren wasteland? A sad-looking lawn detracts from the entire scenario. If your lawn is ready for a redo, consider why it looks so bad now. You'll want to create a lawn that lasts.

> **The topography.** If your home sits on a slope or otherwise challenging lot, what's being done to turn that into an asset rather than a shortcoming?

List the Ups and Downs

Finish your curbside review with a look around to determine "keeper" elements—from boulders that aren't going anywhere without a bulldozer to mature trees that add shade and beauty. Be sure to include elements such as pretty window boxes in your plan, too. Then move on to a list of landscape "remedy me" elements, such as a patchy lawn or overgrown border. Consider what needs to be repaired and put those items high on the list.

RIGHT: The placement of trees and plantings is pivotal for creating an attractive front yard. This cement sidewalk lined with shrubs beckons visitors to the front door.

Watch video on how to spruce up your home's exterior at HGTV.com/curbappeal.

CURB APPEAL COMMENT: Rise to the Occasion

Sloping and hilly lots often get an undue bad rap. If your house sits tall, make it stand proud with good design and welcoming steps.

Dream a Little Dream

Take a breather and stop dissecting your home sweet home for a bit. Play time traveler instead and think back to what you first loved about your house. What potential did you see when you bought it?

Now is the time to play up the positives and dream. To create your wish list, flip through this book and mark pages with houses that have a look you like. Drive around the neighborhood and pick out homes that resonate with you and those that resemble your house. Ask yourself: What's the appeal?

As you're searching write down the adjectives and details that come to mind. Buy magazines and clip the pages of homes and yards that catch your eye, circling your favorite elements.

Keep an eye on the practical as you collect ideas. Ask yourself what you, your kids, and your pets need in a front yard, and what level of maintenance is appealing to you. After all, grounding your expectations in reality is the straightest path to happily ever after.

The Majors vs. The Minors

Turn "can't imagines" into "can-dos" by bringing down the volume on your makeover aspirations. These little facelifts are great alternatives to serious overhauls and can pack as much visual punch from the curb:

Major	Minor
New porch	New railings
New windows	New shutters, trim paint
New siding, overall	New trim color, fresh paint
New door	Newly painted door
New portico	New awning
New slate roof	New faux slate roof
New drive	Newly stained concrete
New landscaping	New container plants and window boxes
New exterior paint job	Newly painted trim and accents
New outdoor lighting	New porch light
New fence	New arbor
New waterfalls	New water fountain
New fish pond	New container water garden
New custom finishings	New Internet and salvage finds
Designer and contractors	Books, magazines, software, and DIY

ABOVE: Think back to when you first saw your house. What attracted you to the style? What ideas came to mind that you wanted to implement someday? Those ideas can form the basis of your homefront makeover.

CURB APPEAL COMMENT: Be a Team Player

Unless your spouse, partner, or roommate has given you free rein, be sure to include them in the redesign process. Get buy-in from your home team, and they're more likely to pitch in to help.

Create a Blank Canvas

On *Curb Appeal*, the designers show viewers sketches of the featured homes void of the existing problems and dressed in the solutions. A similar coloring-book-style rendering is essential to envision your "after" changes in context.

To get a personalized sketch of your own house, you can go high tech with makeover software available online or at local home improvement and office supply chains. Or you can go low tech with pencil and paper. Since we're all about simplicity and saving money, here's the low-tech approach:

> **Take a straight-on photo of your house.** (Digital shots are ideal.) Enlarge the photo to fill a sheet of letter- or legal-size paper, and make a print out.

> **Cover that image with tracing paper.** Using a dark pencil or pen, trace the outline of the house and any hardscape structures that will remain in your "after."

Sketch Out a Site Plan As you move beyond the assess-and-dream phase, you'll want a site plan to complement your curb-view rendering. An overhead view of your property, a site plan helps you lay out elements such as the drive, paths, and landscaping. Ideally you can obtain copies of your house and property map (called a plat) from your local tax assessor's office and fill them in as directed in later chapters. Or follow these steps for an approximation:

1. Measure your lot and draw it on a sheet of paper to scale. (One-fourth—100 feet of property to 25 inches of paper—is a standard conversion. If you're stuck, an architect's ruler might simplify things.)

2. Include slope by holding a leveled board or yardstick at the top of the slope. Measure the distance from the suspended end of the stick to the ground, known as the rise. Divide the run (the length of your board) by the rise to get the slope's grade, or the percentage of drop. Continue measuring the slope until you get to the property boundary, or until the ground levels again. Note the run and the slope's grade changes on your site plan.

3. Place your accurately measured house on the lot, in the proper place. (Since we're focusing on curb appeal, you can skip the back of the house.)

4. Measure and sketch in the hardscape features you plan to keep, such as the drive and walkways. To map out curves, pick a straight line (a wall, a fence, etc.), and use it as your base, measuring the distance between it and the curved element at several points. These series points form a line.

5. Add in keeper landscape elements, like trees and plant beds.

LEFT: As you compose your site plan, don't sweat the measurements too much. The idea is to create a proportional rendering to give you an idea of what you can fit in the space you have.

ABOVE: As you continue planning your exterior overhaul, remember to make note of elements you admire on other homes. Even the look of a neighbor's house numbers, window boxes, or potted plants may inspire you.

CURB APPEAL COMMENT: Have Some Fun

Using colored pencils and landscaping templates will help you create a design that more closely resembles the end result. Templates and a wide variety of pencil colors are available at art supply stores.

Stay Organized You can use a three-ring binder to ensure your makeover doesn't become a three-ring circus! Keep your pro-and-con lists, dream tear sheets, schedules, budgets—everything related to the project—to track the progress and expenses. Don't forget to add before and after photos to create a brag book for when friends visit, or when you show the home to buyers in the future.

> **Trace any existing architectural details** (shutters, windows, porches) that will remain. Also trace any existing landscape details you'll keep.

> **Make several copies of the final tracing, which will act as your blank slate from here after.**

As you develop your plan, you'll continue to add elements such as color and plantings to this rendering. If you do that as you follow this book, in the end you'll have a completed rendering—a master plan for your own curb appeal remodeling.

Always keep at least one copy of the original drawing as a "master" copy—otherwise no doubt you'll have your best idea just after you've scribbled all over your last copy. On the copies, you'll be trying out different scenarios. Even if you don't like a drawing as it develops, keep it in a separate file until the end. You might not like the color on one copy, for example, but the idea you had for a gate on that one may have been your best.

ABOVE: See how new details on the Carroll/Gross home, which was featured on *Curb Appeal*, add style to the plain facade. Using a photo of your home and layering on the ideas will help you envision the effects of proposed changes. (P.S. Turn to page 22 to see the final results of this makeover.)

HOUSE RENDER REMINDER
Don't leave Chapter One without a rough rendering of your house and front yard as seen from the curb. (See page 16.)

Cost Benefits

If you're feeling over-whelmed—
or under-financed—for tackling
curb appeal improvements,
ponder this: Studies indicate that
a great landscape can up your
home's value between 7 to 15
percent; a great paint job can add
as much as 10 percent. Talk about
payoff—and motivation!

Take Time for the Bottom Line

Chances are you're not blessed with bottomless pockets. If you're like most people and have to look at a restaurant bill before you sign off on the receipt, pause for a moment to consider budget up front.

To get a feel for the cost of every project you're considering, call local nurseries, garden centers, and home improvement stores for tool and supply prices, or search online. Home improvement veterans suggest you double your estimated total project costs to allow wiggle room for missteps and pesky realities.

A different approach entails gathering ballpark estimates for professional services. If you're a die-hard do-it-yourselfer with access to the necessary tools, you can typically cut those quotes in half. Regardless of who does the work at hand, let your budget guide you through your makeover. Be sure to set a reasonable work pace that doesn't overwhelm you—or your bank account.

Because your home improvement isn't being photographed for television, you can create a "layered" plan where you take on—and pay for—one part of the project at a time. Another way to stretch your budget is to find creative, budget-savvy alternatives for the big-ticket items on your dream plan. See The Majors vs. The Minors (page 14) for some budget-wise tricks.

Set Up a Timeline

Even in the hyper-accelerated world of television production, designers and contractors depend on timelines to make those stunning "afters" a reality. Follow suit and think of your own timeline as the strategy to bring your dreams to life, whether it takes a Saturday, a weekend, or a few months.

First, outline the overarching projects that have made it to your to-do list. (You'll likely only know this after your final rendering is filled in and completed.)

Next, assign an estimated project rating beside each overall project. Put repair work as the top priority and then, since schedules and budgets go hand-in-hand, let your finances and logic dictate the remaining order. Perhaps you have saved up to have a score of projects hammered out at once, or maybe you're willing to take out a loan. On the other hand, you might want to set aside a monthly allowance. Or you could be the type who checks out what leftover cash you have this week, and determines how far it'll stretch based on your dream Dos.

Finally, whatever your approach, make sure you put one foot in front of the other, laying down walkways, for example, before you plant your landscape, and painting the house before you pick out your new fixtures and flowers.

POSITE: Take your exterior
model one step at a time. If your
ch is falling down, make building
ew one your top priority.

ABOVE: If you can't afford a
complete overhaul, improving
landscaping and lighting can boost
curb appeal cost effectively.

BEFORE

AFTER

HERE'S WHAT THEY DID

Jim Gross and Bridgette Carroll's tiny 120-year-old Victorian cottage had fixer-upper written all over it. But the sporty couple is more into tackling the outdoors than tackling a restoration project. So *Curb Appeal* designer Tom Leach did his historical homework and came up with exterior details that turned the place from a present-day eyesore into a throwback showstopper.

The results are an homage to the home's era and are easy to care for—particularly because the exterior is tricked out with modern materials, such as an MDF (medium-density fiberboard) door and poly-blend materials, which are maintenance-free and won't break the bank.

Before, the house colors—boring, baby-blue with white and red accents—were ill-matched. Now, a combo of winter sky gray and slate blue, offset by trim in white with gold detailing, provides a crisp palette that's very Victorian.

The old front door and its too-small window were replaced with a new, classic reproduction that sports a larger window and overhead transom to allow more light inside the house.

Where before only the fish-scale shingles and one pair of roof brackets lent a Victorian feel to the home, now a door awning, window cornices with an elaborate supporting cast of brackets and thick trim, plus beveled panels and medallion accents make the house a true Victorian gem.

Replacing the tiny windows and their rotting frames was a big step toward overcoming the house's squatty look. The new, larger windows create the illusion of added height. Double-pane glass with tilting, removable sashes makes cleaning easy and increases the energy and sound insulation.

To finish the exterior remodel in style, a new deck offers a place for chairs and potted plants, including the iron-finished urns filled with drought-resistant palms that flank the door—another element en vogue during Victorian days.

A Victorian-replica mailbox and gold, Victorian-style house numbers painted on the transom add stop-in-your-tracks bold and beautiful finishing touches.

Photo Details >>>

1: Brackets, thick trim, beveled panels, and medallion accents echo Victorian style.
2: A period-proper milk glass light fixture illuminates the front door.
3: Thick white trim accented in blue and gold creates an elegantly subdued look.
4: Finishing elements, including iron-finished urns and a replica mailbox, provide the perfect finishing details.

Whether you're a Victorian period buff or sitting on your own vintage diamond in the rough, check out these updates to restore your house to newfound glory days.

Before: Tiny windows with rotting frames **After:** Vertically oriented windows with double-pane glass, window cornices, and thick trim **Before:** An old front door more last-century ranch than Victorian	**After:** A classic reproduction door with a glass window that echoes the shape of the exterior windows **Before:** A lack of true Victorian elements **After:** A door awning, window cornices, thick trim, beveled panels,	medallion accents, and fish-scale shingles **Before:** A dilapidated fence hiding the house **After:** A new deck made of easy-care cedar that serves as an outdoor addition

2

DRESS UP THE HOUSE

Create Fantastic Front Entries, Dynamite Doorways, and Windows with Wow!

Ever notice how some houses seem to wink at passersby? That's because they have the basics down—a great entry, nicely dressed windows, and a tip-top rooftop—all of which add up to a home's persona. From the curb, it's that character that invites homeowners in at the end of the day, and it's what welcomes guests when they drop by. If your house could use a little coaching in the personality department, a *Curb Appeal* makeover will take it from lackluster wallflower to Miss Congeniality faster than you can say "belle of the ball." Here you'll find out how to inject a little life into your home's most prominent features, because little things really do mean a lot.

Fancy Front Entrances

The first thing your eye seeks when scanning a house is a way in, and given the importance of front entrances, show designers always focus there first. Follow their lead and study your entryway from the sidewalk or curb.

Take a look at the doorway dressings, grouped here by landings, overhangs, and doors. Define the good, the bad, and the ugly, and read on for remedies that will take your exterior from drab to fab.

Enticing Entryways: Here's What to Do

I need ... A set of stairs or steps that are not too steep and are wide enough for two. Create new steps with treads that are 3 feet or more wide and at least 1 foot deep; risers should be between 4 and 7 inches high.

I need ... A space to greet people at the front door. Add a small stoop that is large enough for two people.

I need ... A place to put container plants and to sit a spell. Make a landing big enough to accommodate seating.

I need ... A gathering place to convene outdoors and connect with the neighborhood. Build a small porch or expand a front-door landing into a front-yard patio.

> **Lovely landings.** Turn your attention to your front landing itself. If you're happy with its scale and style, inspect the functionality: Are the steps even and in good shape? Is there sufficient room for you and visitors? Are all railings secure? Tend to repairs. Otherwise, problem solve as outlined below, keeping in mind that your house's overall architectural style should dictate your design—modern shapes with modern homes, and hand-hewn looks with Arts and Crafts cottages, for example.

LEFT: Clearing out crowded shrubs and bumping out the entryway leaves room for a friendly front door, spacious steps, and plenty of space to greet guests.

ABOVE: Set the entry into the front of the house to define the area and keep the facade smooth—a good choice for homes with a modern look.

CURB APPEAL COMMENT: Make an Attention-Grabber

ABOVE: Although it's not the first element of the exterior to greet company, this masterfully designed entrance is bound to steal guests' attention away from the garage.

A clear path and distinct architecture will make an entryway stand out—even if the garage is the most prominent feature on a house.

> **Oh-la-la overhangs.** After you settle on the best landing, tune into what's overhead, also known as the overhang. A front-door overhang can be as simple as a fabric canopy or as major as a massive portico, and what works for your house depends on your needs, your budget, and—as always—the architecture. Take your cue from the bone structure of the house: Look at the rendering you made in Chapter One, and echo or contrast the roofline. Is your house boxy with a flat roof? A rounded canvas awning might soften the look and complement its crisp lines. Is your house a cottage with a steeply pitched roof? A small portico that echoes existing gables could give the whole house a polished look.

> **Captivating columns.** Columns standing guard around a front door announce the entrance to a home. Sometimes, columns are meant for looks alone. Other times, they serve as load-bearing supports. It's critical to know which type you have before tampering with existing models. Many last-century ranch and colonial houses sport thin scrolls of ironwork meant to represent columns. Adding the real deal might be just the anchor your entrance needs to modernize and even out proportions.

Awesome Alternatives

If you've run the numbers and searched high and low but overhangs and columns are still budget breakers, consider these alternatives to economically achieve the same effect:

Arbors: Two side trellises connected by a top, arbors are made of wood, metal, or vinyl. Install one to frame a front door. Train vines to grow over the trellises to create a lush, green entrance.

Faux pediments and friezes: These decorative moldings distinguish a front door in the way a portico frames an entrance. Faux moldings mimic gabled cornices and full-size friezes and barely protrude from a house facade.

Pergolas: Mount the roof of a pergola—a formal wood structure made of heavy carved posts and beams—over a door for an alternative, airy overhang.

Pilasters: All the style of a column without the bulk, flat pilasters attach directly to exterior walls.

Shutters: Mount them on either side of the front door for visual significance. Make sure shutters are proportional (the full height of your front door, and half its width), and painted in harmony with window shutters and the rest of the house.

Trellises: Flank the front door with a pair of trellises to impersonate formal columns.

TOP LEFT: A simple portico topped with a Chippendale-style railing gives a standard home a stylish street presence.

LEFT: Shutters mounted on either side of these French doors add visual significance.

OPPOSITE: A copper-top portico and classic white columns add dimension to this New England-style home.

HOUSE RENDER REMINDER
Sketch your dream dressings—windows, entrances, and doors—onto your house rendering. Color the roof accordingly.

23

Visit HGTV.com/howtodemos for animated step-by-step projects for doors, windows and more.

Fantastic Front Doors

A front door greets anyone who crosses your threshold, so make yours a bold standout that welcomes visitors. Know money spent here are dollars easily recouped, as the most basic front door makeover ups curb appeal exponentially.

Give your door a thorough inspection and ask yourself design, style, and condition questions to determine if you'll keep it as is, update it a little, or replace it altogether.

> **It's a keeper.** Does your front door hardware work properly, does it look sharp with the rest of the house details, and is it in overall good condition? If so, lucky you. Clean the door, perhaps give it a fresh coat of paint along with the rest of the house, and check it off your makeover to-do list.

> **Next! Replacement time.** Stroll through a home improvement center and it's obvious there are more types of front doors than Smiths in a phone book. Settle on the general style (double or single doors, glass or solid), the extemporaneous architectural and design elements (transoms, sidelights, pilasters), and concerns (safety, energy efficiency), then shop by material.

- **Clad:** Wood on the inside and covered (or clad) in metal, vinyl, or polyester, clad doors marry synthetic and natural components, boasting the best of both.
- **Fiberglass:** Like vinyl doors, fiberglass models are lightweight and easy to install, but unlike vinyl, they can be stained similar to wood.
- **Metal:** Nearly maintenance-free, aluminum and steel doors have foam cores for energy efficiency. The array of colors and grainlike detail readily mimic wood.
- **Vinyl:** With minimal cost and care, paint-'n'-go vinyl doors suit any house color scheme. They, too, have faux wood grain detailing. The downside? You can't stain them.
- **Wood:** Nostalgia places wood doors in high regard, but sentimentality has a price. Wood is energy efficient and weathers with style, but it requires refinishing and suffers from shrinking and swelling. Opt for treated varieties for the best results.

Update Me, Please

If your front door itself is fine but could use a facelift or a tune-up, try these ideas for a fresh look:
- Add new hardware, such as a handle, door knocker, kickplate, and hinges
- Attach new weather stripping
- Cut a window into the door
- Insert sidelights
- Pop in a transom

CURB APPEAL COMMENT: Downsize To Up Appeal

Is a pair of double doors overwhelming your home, making it appear overly formal? Replace the two with a single door.

Wonderful Windows

If a person's eyes are the windows to the soul, then a house's windows open to its soul. Glance at any building: Windows are spellbinding in how they break up a facade, reflect the outside world, and frame interior scenes.

As such, new or revitalized windows do wonders to freshen up any abode. Read on to make those peepers sparkle.

> **Not too late to update.** If your windows allow costly cooled and heated air to escape, or are beyond simple repairs, you still have a few options before starting from scratch. To improve efficiency, add storm windows, apply window film, or use insulating window treatments. If the frames are in good condition, but the windows themselves are not, install replacement windows, available through home improvement centers and specialty stores. These slip into existing frames, can be custom-fit to your needs, and are relatively easy to install yourself, which balances out the expense. If such updates still won't solve the problems at hand, use your situation as the perfect opportunity to switch to a whole new style, size, and shape.

ABOVE: The colorful window frames of this Mediterranean Revival home complement its stucco walls.

Know Your Numbe

New windows earn grade based on ratings that measure the heat that fl through (U-value) and S Heat Gain Coefficiency (SHGC), the air that pass from outside to inside an vice versa. For optimum performance, look for U-value ratings of .35 or less, and SHGC ratings of .4 or less.

ABOVE: These sleek windows don't require shutters. The new central window serves as a focal point and offers great views of the yard and wooded area beyond. The smartly chosen window style includes muntins to break up the large span of glass and fit the home's style.

Glazing Know-How

A builder's term for what layfolk call glass, glazing is key to an energy-efficient window. Here's what's available.

Double-pane glazing: Two sheets of glass with an air pocket sandwiched in the middle, making it twice as efficient as a single pane.

Triple-pane glazing: Triples single-pane efficiency with three panes and two air pockets.

Argon-filled glazing: A double-pane window with argon in the middle for three times the efficiency of a single pane.

Low-E glazing: Glass is coated with oxides to block most UV and all infrared light, which helps keep houses toasty in the winter and cool in the summer.

Tempered and laminated glazing: A tough, impact-resistant glass, thus a good choice for coastal homes and for heavily used elements like doors.

Steps to a Shipshape Window Revival

If your old windows are salvageable, here's how to get them back into shipshape condition. (Be careful to control the force used to scrape, sand, and prep, as you want to preserve the glass and framing.)

Step One: Remove trim and other decorative elements that don't pass muster.

Step Two: Strip any chipped, peeling, or otherwise damaged paint using scrapers, heat guns, putty knives, etc.

Step Three: Remove and replace broken glazing, glass, and muntins.

Step Four: If the old glazing compound is in pieces, remove the remaining chunks. If the old glazing compound is only moderately cracked, continue to the next step.

Step Five: Prep surfaces for painting as described in Chapter Three. Use steel wool on metals and sandpaper on wood.

Step Six: Repair holes, mend cracks, and newly seal or reinforce glazing with fresh glazing compound and caulking as needed.

Step Seven: Let new sealants dry, add new trim, then paint.

RIGHT: The squares of this stained-glass window located just below the roofline echo the shape of the rest of the home's windows.

> **New windows, new world.** Refer to the wish list you came up with in Chapter One. Are you happy with the placement of your existing windows? Do you crave more light inside your home, or a view to the front? Study the windows on other houses similar to yours for combinations and layouts you admire. Daydream a little, using your house rendering to sketch out a few options. Take your illustration to an architect or designer who will draw up final plans, and enlist a licensed contractor to execute the changes.

Details That Delight

Some homeowners think that an easy-to-clean, easy-to-use window is priceless. If you count yourself in those ranks, be prepared to shell out more for your fantasy windows. Look for tilting sashes and removable grilles or muntins that allow for easy cleaning; hidden casements and awnings; window cranks; and models with dust-free blinds built in between double panes.

CURB APPEAL COMMENT: Follow the Leader

A good redesign rule is to match new windows to the style of predominant existing windows, and align the tops of windows on the same floor.

Casements and Awnings and Gliders—Oh My!

Half of getting what you want is knowing what to ask for. When it comes to changing out windows, brush up on the lingo to score success. Below you'll find the most popular types available today:

Awning: Top-hinged and hand-cranked to pivot open, horizontally oriented awnings are similar to casements, but don't open as fully. Suited for: Ranches, prairie-style, contemporary homes.

Casement: Tall, narrow windows, casements are side-hinged and hand-cranked to pivot open fully. Add muntins to make casements appear more traditional. Suited for: Ranches, prairie-style, contemporary homes.

Double- and single-hung: Classic windows with muntins and a pair of movable sashes that slide vertically to open and close. (In single-hung windows, only the lower sash moves.) Suited for: Cape Cods, Colonials, Victorians, 20th-century bungalows, period homes.

Gliding: Similar to sliding glass doors, gliding windows slide horizontally along their frame's tracks. Suited for: Ranches, prairie-style, contemporary homes.

Picture: Stationary windows that don't open, picture windows are so-called because they are meant to maximize views. Suited for: Cape Cods, Colonials, Victorians, 20th-century bungalows, period homes (small versions, with muntins), contemporary styles (large versions, without muntins).

Specialty Windows: Triangular, circular, crescent, or pie-wedged, specialty windows typically don't open and are meant to add an artistic flair to a home. (Can also include stained glass and other leaded glass in a variety of shapes and styles.) Suited for: Cape Cods, Colonials, Victorians, 20th-century bungalows, period homes.

> **Functional frames.** Frames hold windows in place and seal your home's inner and outer walls. They are integral to preventing (or contributing to) water damage and energy efficiency problems. Plus, frames are visible from the inside of your home, so your choice of material is well worth deliberating.

- Aluminum frames cost less than wood frames, but don't perform well in cold climates. They also require tender handling as they scratch and dent easily.

- Fiberglass frames offer the best qualities of all framing materials, and are therefore the priciest.

- Vinyl-clad frames weather extremely well and have great energy-saving performance, but 100 percent vinyl frames are not as structurally sound and sturdy as other materials. However, builders can shore up all-vinyl frames with inserts.

- Wood composite frames—a blend of wood fiber and plastics—are usually clad in vinyl or aluminum, are strong, and have sound energy efficiency. Stain finishes are not an option.

- Wood frames, typically clad in waterproof sheathing, are good insulators. But they shrink or swell depending on the weather and need periodic upkeep.

ABOVE: An open casement window framed by shutters lets in plenty of light and fresh air.

OPPOSITE TOP: A variety of window sizes, shapes, and styles lend understated style.

OPPOSITE BOTTOM: Colorful shutters frame a casement window.

Stretch Those Window Dollars

If you're a caviar person on a fish-fry budget, windows with all the bells and whistles are probably out of the question. But don't despair. Try these workarounds to come out on top without going broke:

• Skip custom-size and shape windows. Instead, adjust your rough opening to suit stock standards, which are usually measured in variables of 2 and 4 inches.

• Find out which of the pricey varieties are most plentiful in stock where you shop specially ordered models up your costs.

• Pass on Low-E coated windows on the shaded side of your house because it needs less sun protection.

• Install windows yourself to save contractor costs. Or, if you have two stories, tackle the first floor then hire out the remaining work.

Right-On Roofs

Replacing a roof is a costly undertaking and is usually more about leaks than looks. But if you decide it's turnover time for your house topper, know that the more gables, dormers, chimneys, and skylights your house wears, the more roof installation will cost.

Roofing Options

Asphalt (average- to high-quality) **Pros:** Lightweight; inexpensive; easy to install and replace. Fire resistance varies widely. **Cons:** May not pass all building codes. **Lifespan:** 15–50 years **Cost:** $50–$100 per sq. ft. installed.

Cedar Shakes Pros: Natural look; lightweight; earthy color and texture. **Cons:** Must be treated to be fire-retardant; roof pitch must be 4 to 12 inches or more. **Lifespan:** 25–50 years **Cost:** $150–$225 per sq. ft. installed.

Clay Tile Pros: Variety of colorful looks; resistant to rot, moisture, and fire. **Cons:** Expensive; extremely heavy. **Lifespan:** 50 years **Cost:** $350–$450 per sq. ft. installed.

Concrete Tile Pros: Resistant to rot, moisture, and fire; medium-weight. **Cons:** Moss and mildew can grow on concrete tile in warm, wet climates. **Lifespan:** 50 years **Cost:** $150–$250 per sq. ft. installed.

Slate Pros: Resistant to rot, moisture, and fire; long lifespan. **Cons:** Expensive to buy, install, and repair; heavy. **Lifespan:** 50–100 years **Cost:** $500–$750 per sq. ft. installed.

Standing Seam Steel Pros: Wind- and fire-resistant; lightweight; can cut home insurance costs. **Cons:** Corrosion with untreated metal; hail damage can occur with uncoated metal. **Lifespan:** 25–50 years **Cost:** $250–$400 per sq. ft. installed.

OPPOSITE: Regardless of which type of material you choose, remember that a varied roofline will up the cost of your roof installation dramatically.

Do It Yourself or Hire a Pro? Wondering if you have the stuff it takes to tackle the projects that sprucing up your windows, entrances, and roofs entail? Check out this advice to help you decide.

If you're the household handyperson ... Then you can remove and install a window—especially the kit types.

If you dream of an arbor over your front door ... Then go for it! This project is super-simple when you buy premade arbors.

If an alteration necessitates cutting into your house facade or roof ... Then hire a pro to make sound design and structural decisions.

If you're considering anything but asphalt tile on your roof ... Then stick with a contractor; they are insured against mishaps and will repair any problems that crop up with the first rainy season.

BEFORE

AFTER

Photo Details >>>

1: Sandblasted glass on the door and transom replicate the frosted glass on the Asian-inspired gate.
2: Hiding a bubble skylight behind cedar planking and adding a Japanese-style railing to the balcony were two upper-level improvements.
3: For a natural look, new red cedar planking covers the body of the house.
4: The soothing Zen garden includes a bamboo fountain and cedar bench.

HERE'S WHAT THEY DID

In order to stay sane after a hectic day at their high-pressure jobs, homeowners Lisa Chadwick and Ian Schmidt turn to yoga to unwind. So when Lisa and Ian decided their boxy, boring house needed improvement, an Asian aesthetic was the natural choice.

Designer Kem Theilig and landscape designer Daniel Owens were enlisted to help. It was painfully obvious what had to go—the faded '70s shingles, bad retro entry, and out of control yard were a far cry from soothing.

For the body of the house, Kem chose red cedar planking over painted metal for a modern, natural look. The same planking covers the walls that separate the property from the neighbors' yard and serves as a partition to hide the awkward bubble skylight above the entry.

Replacing the upper balcony's jail-like railing in favor of one constructed from traditional Japanese wood furthered the Asian aesthetic. The windows and doors feature beige-painted wood trim. A new front door and sidelight match the style of the Asian-inspired gate—the glass in both the door and gate is frosted for privacy and visual interest. Cedar planters, handmade clay tiles on the front

steps, and stainless-steel details includi metallic house numbers and a mailb complete the entry.

The once-unruly front yard has be transformed into a Zen garden compl with bamboo and other Asian plants. limestone path leads to the garden, wh a new cedar bench provides the perf perch for enjoying the soothing sound water trickle from a bamboo spout.

Glean some ideas from this Asian-inspired *Curb Appeal* update to create your own place to call "ohm."

Before: A boring, boxy exterior with a dark color scheme
After: Contemporary red cedar siding

Before: Out-of-control plantings and nowhere to sit

After: Simple plantings, serene stonework, and a red cedar bench

Before: An unwelcoming entry
After: Cool clay tiles, a frosted glass door, and metallic details

Before: Outdated windows and French doors
After: Simple windows and doors with rich beige trim

3

COLOR YOUR WORLD

Paint Your Way to Perfection

Ahhh, color: It's the head-turner that sets your imagination off and running, and incites everything from sentimentality to plain old passion. No wonder such an inspiring element can be a handful to pin down. But don't despair— every last one of us manages to coordinate our clothes each day, and settling on what your house will wear is not all that different. Tune into this insider know-how from show experts to determine your dream color scheme, learn what colors to paint where, and discover tips on how to wield a paintbrush like a pro. After all, a fresh wash of color is one of the easiest ways to instantly up your home's curb appeal, and it's the fastest ticket to a major impact makeover.

Color by Numbers

Choosing your color scheme is simple. Take a walk around your neighborhood and you'll see the typical formula: House body, one color; trim, another color; shutters, a third color; and, occasionally, doors, a fourth.

To dress your house up in your personal color palette, follow these simple steps.

Step One: Take the color quiz (page 54) to learn your ideal palette.

Step Two: Take out several copies of the traced renderings of your house from Chapter One.

Step Three: Color in the fixed elements, such as the roof, awnings, foundation, and any stone or brickwork that will remain as is.

Step Four: Pick possible color schemes and color in your drawing with those combinations until you settle on a combination that ultimately looks—and feels—right.

Step Five: Take your finished drawing to a paint store (bring an actual photo of your house, too). Ask a sales clerk for the shades closest to the ones you've settled on,

and buy quart-sized samples of each.

Step Six: Paint a swath of each color on your house. (The street-frontage side is the best, but if you're modest, try testing on the sides or back.)

Step Seven: Live with the sample colors a few days to see how the sun and shadow affects the hues.

Step Eight: Make your final choice and order your paint.

ABOVE AND LEFT: After examining possible color schemes and settling on the best combination, paint a swath of each color on your house to see if the hues are really what you want.

OPPOSITE: This home's color scheme reflects the sky, water, and beach. The montage of blues and beige is broken up by white trim.

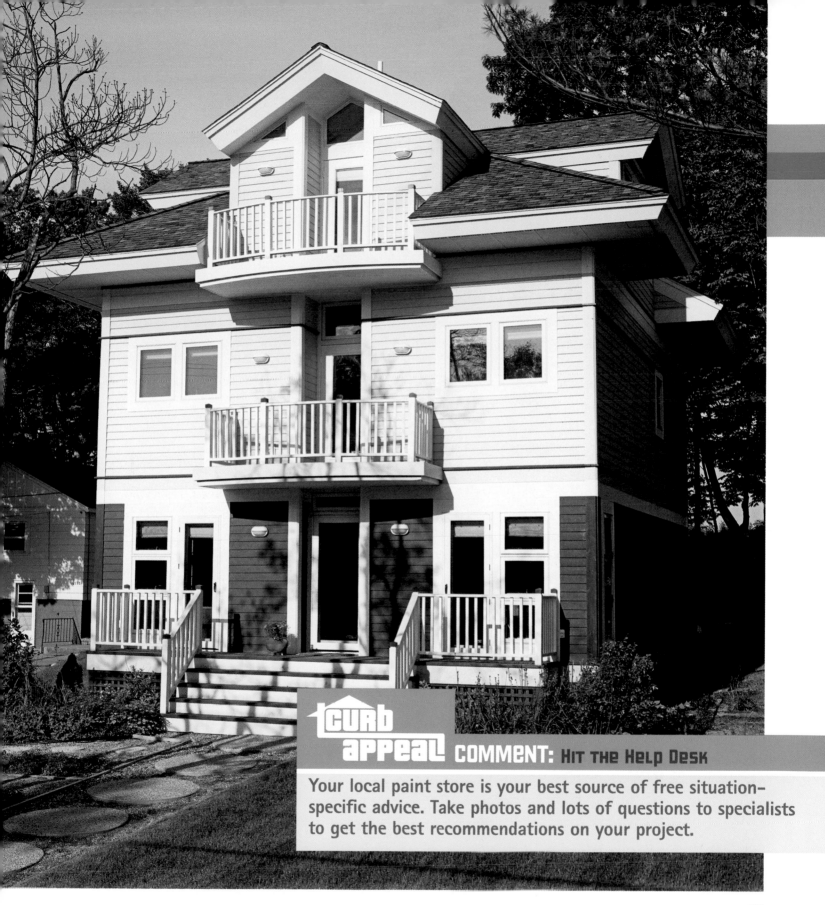

CURB APPEAL COMMENT: Hit the Help Desk

Your local paint store is your best source of free situation-specific advice. Take photos and lots of questions to specialists to get the best recommendations on your project.

Determine Your Dream-Team Color Scheme

Designers may work some magic on *Curb Appeal*, but they don't pull their color suggestions out of thin air. Use their cache of tricks of the trade—color wheels, paint chip strips, and trial and error—to find optimum palettes.

Get in on their game and take heed of these tried-and-true tips that lead them to success.

> **Pair roof and house colors.** Black and gray roofs look great with nearly all house colors, while orange tile roofs work best with earth tones. Strong-color roofs (like red and green) team well with light shades of yellow and green, while tan and white houses complement any roof color.

> **Use dark colors** to make a house look smaller and more intimate. Use light colors to make a house seem larger.

> **Choose colors that complement** the "keeper" flowers, trees, and shrubs in your yard. Stay in the same color family to blend into your lot, or use complementary contrasting colors to show off your Eden. If your yard is minimal and the closest outdoor elements are your neighbors' homes, play off their colors.

> **Paint shutters and doors with contrast** in mind. If your house is pale or medium, opt for a dark shutter color; if it's dark, consider a bright color.

> **Use trim paint to accentuate** a house's overall body lines and its architectural details. For example, paint vents, windows, railings, balconies, and columns the same color as your trim.

> **Highlight extra elements.** Arbors and gazebos stand out when painted in a highlight color.

> **Camouflage gutters.** Paint gutters the color of trim, and hide downspouts by painting them in the same color as the house facade, be it wood, brick, or stone.

> **Make small windows appear larger** and more inviting with light trim. Make big windows, and houses

Beginning on page 47 and continuing through page 53, you'll see homes that suffer from common color problems, as well as the results of complete color makeovers that make them shine. Take cues from these color corrections to select the perfect hues for your color update.

LEFT: Look to your home's architectural style for color palette cues. Victorian and other ornate home styles handle vibrant and contrasting color schemes better than more subdued designs.

body

trim

accent

ABOVE: This ranch home looked like a layer cake. Its roof, siding, and brick divided the facade and provided no focal point. Furthermore, the bland color scheme hid the windows and front door—the home's prettiest features. Now, the khaki-hue body color is a pleasing companion to the brick, and it minimizes the appearance of the layers. The creamy off-white trim defines the charming windows and makes them appear larger. Adding dark gray-green fascia and gutter accents creates an outline that directs the eye down. A ruddy-hue front door becomes the facade's centerpiece.

An analogous color scheme (such as blues and greens) is often used on exteriors. Another option is complementary contrasting, which involves colors that look good together but are distinctly different, such as chocolate brown and pale blue.

overwhelmed with scores of them, seem cozier and smaller with dark trim.

> **Play down stairs by painting** them the color of the porch or landing. Dress them up by painting the stair treads gray, and the risers—the slats that face outward—white, or the color of your trim.

> **Use light or medium shades of gray** on high-traffic floors, such as porch floors and stair treads—that's often the color of industrial-strength floor paint, so it's an easy choice. Or try dark green—a common color to tie a house to the ground—on foundations, and continue that shade on the porch and stairs as well.

Do It Yourself or Hire a Pro?

Curb Appeal homeowners split the workload with designers, contractors, and crew. To decide if you need to make your color redesign a team effort, consider these situations:

If you can coordinate your wardrobe or an interior room ... Then you can choose a great color scheme for your house.

If you can paint an interior room ... Then you can paint a one-story dwelling.

If you're not afraid of heights, and have patience, time, and the right equipment ... Then you can paint nearly any house.

If you have a home loaded with embellishments (like an ornate Victorian gingerbread house) ... Then hire a designer to determine what color scheme to use and how to best play up the details.

If you find yourself planning to use more than four colors ... Then you're in pro territory; consider a color consultation to confirm—or tone down—your selections.

If prepping your house exposes big problems (massive rot, excessive mildew, rusted metal siding, significant cracks) ... Then hire a contractor to do repair and cleaning work before they—or you—paint.

If you don't have the time, tools, and stamina for a full-house paint job ... Then enlist a professional; the sidestepped stress is worth the price in the end.

If you can't afford outsourcing all the work ... Then consult with the pros to see how to split the workload between you and them.

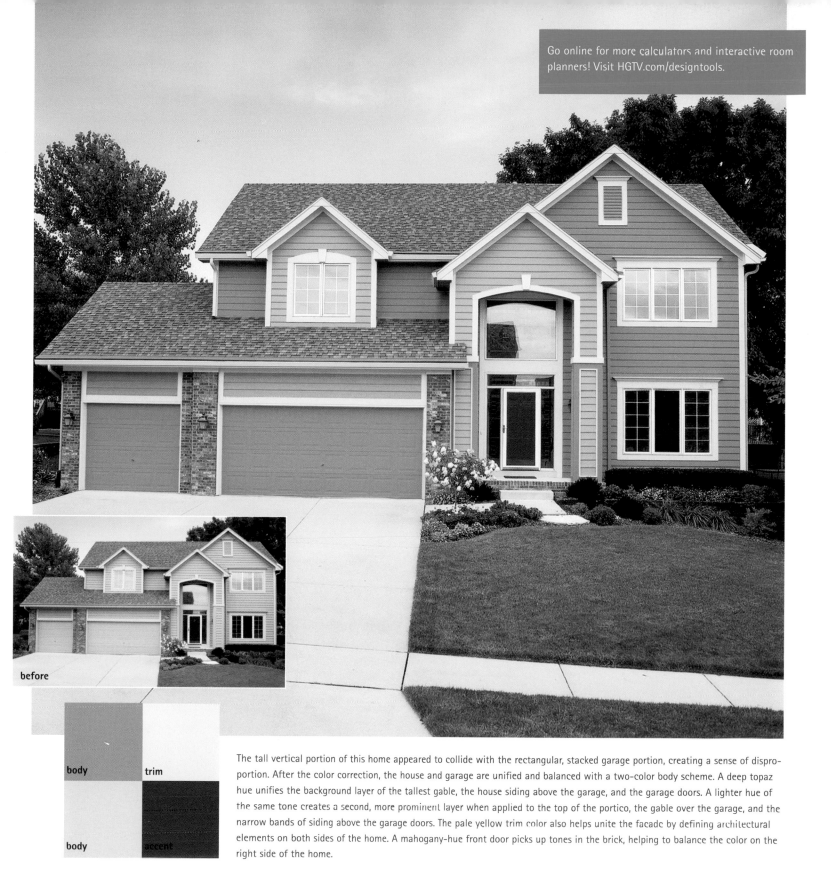

Go online for more calculators and interactive room planners! Visit HGTV.com/designtools.

before

| body | trim |
| body | accent |

The tall vertical portion of this home appeared to collide with the rectangular, stacked garage portion, creating a sense of disproportion. After the color correction, the house and garage are unified and balanced with a two-color body scheme. A deep topaz hue unifies the background layer of the tallest gable, the house siding above the garage, and the garage doors. A lighter hue of the same tone creates a second, more prominent layer when applied to the top of the portico, the gable over the garage, and the narrow bands of siding above the garage doors. The pale yellow trim color also helps unite the facade by defining architectural elements on both sides of the home. A mahogany-hue front door picks up tones in the brick, helping to balance the color on the right side of the home.

Pull Out Your Paintbrush

Pulling out the brushes and opening the cans are actually the last steps you take when painting your house. The prep work that leads up to that finale is essential, makes the job go smoothly, and protects your overall investment—dollars and sweat equity included.

The goal is to create a clean, dry, and smooth canvas for the final coat, so play the role of diligent homeowner, minding the Dos below. When brush time rolls around, choose a string of mild-temperature, clear- or hazy-skied days, because when the weather is too cold, paint tends to adhere poorly, and if it's too hot, it can dry too fast—both situations that lead to inconsistent finishes and coloring.

> **Get good and clean.** Clear your house of all dirt and mildew using water and a small amount of household washing detergent. Stubborn mildew requires bleach cleaning—use one part bleach to two parts water to scrub it off, taking care to protect yourself and your plants from the chemicals. For tough jobs, or when time is limited, use a power washer. Follow the directions closely, as you can cause damage if you're not attentive. Avoid power washing bare wood because it absorbs the water, and steer clear of delicate millwork and windows, as both break easily.

> **Smooth things out.** Painting over old, peeling layers makes a fresh paint coat look lumpy, so slough off the old to ensure a slick new look. Scrape boards until they are as smooth as possible, then sand down rough edges, bumps, and irregularities. The goal is to have an even surface on which to paint anew, not to get rid of all of the old color.

> **Repair problem spots.** Neither something as minor as a pockmark, nor something as major as dry or wet rot, should be glossed over, as the problem only worsens over time with a paint patch job. Instead of slapping a coat over trouble areas, fill holes and cracks with caulking, repair windows, and remove and replace rotted woodwork.

CURB APPEAL COMMENT: Strip Down!

Before you paint a house, remove the shutters, then prep and paint them separately.

body

trim

accent

before

This new color scheme softens the once-stark contrast between the home's blue siding, white trim, and tan brick. The original bright blue siding is toned down to a blue-gray hue more complementary to the roof and brick colors. Painting the garage door the same color as the siding helps it recede from view. A warmer white hue for the windows, fascia, and corner boards defines the home's architectural features with subtlety. Dark, smoky-blue accents provide pops of color around the windows and front door to set them apart and lead the eye to these features first.

> **Take time to prime.** Primer is a white or tinted base coat to which subsequent layers of paint adhere easily, thus creating an even look and finish. A must on new wood that's never been painted (or bare old wood), primer also comes in handy when you make a major color change and need to mask a bold "before" shade. Less expensive than regular paint, one coat of primer and a topcoat of the final color can sometimes keep costs down.

> **Paint the right way.** Start painting on the shaded part of your house, as it typically dries slower and yields a more even color than those areas directly in the sun. Finish one major section at a time, following the shade when possible. Paint along the wood grain, going side to side, from top to bottom on horizontal paneling, and up and down from top to bottom on vertical slats. Consider using a power sprayer on porous, uneven surfaces (such as stucco and brick). Allow one coat to dry before painting another.

Five Common Painting Questions

What kind of paint should I use? Latex dries fast and is easy to clean up, so it's a top choice for weekend projects. Use it on brick and other surfaces. Oil adds another day of drying to the process, but provides a better water barrier than latex, and lasts longer. It's best for patient people with water weathering concerns.

When should I stain versus paint? It's a matter of personal preference, but if you have high-quality wood in good condition (cedar or oak, for instance) a stain shows off the natural grain. Also, stains are thinner, cover more area, and thus stretch your dollar. But if you're tired of the natural look, or if your wood is in a rough state, choose paint.

Brush, roller, or both? Again, it's a matter of personal preference, and mostly depends on ease of use. Rollers cover flat (stucco) areas faster, while brushes are great for detailing.

Can I paint vinyl siding? Yes, just prep it as you would wood and make sure your local paint store specialist signs off on the type of paint you buy.

How do I paint metal? Use steel wool (instead of sandpaper) to smooth out aluminum, then run a cloth over it with mineral spirits and paint. Do likewise on galvanized steel, but paint it with specialized latex primer that prevents premature cracking, as metal expands and contracts more readily than other materials. Scrape rust off iron, apply rust converters as an undercoat to prevent further decomposing, and then paint.

Paint Calculator

Use this formula to determine how much paint you will need:

Width of House x Height of House (minus windows and doors) = Exterior Footage

Confirm your estimate by asking your local paint shop pro how much paint you will need to paint your house based on its siding, trim, and size. Get a professional estimate to see if you'll save enough to do the job yourself.

Above: Selecting a color scheme is only the first step in painting your home's exterior.

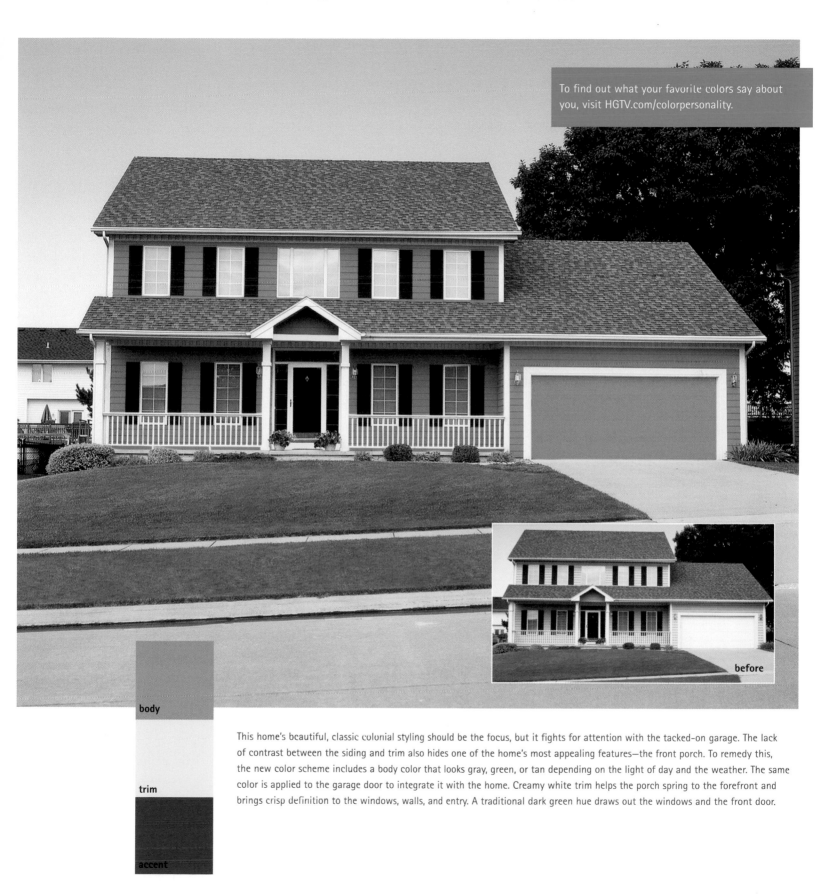

before

body

trim

accent

This home's beautiful, classic colonial styling should be the focus, but it fights for attention with the tacked-on garage. The lack of contrast between the siding and trim also hides one of the home's most appealing features—the front porch. To remedy this, the new color scheme includes a body color that looks gray, green, or tan depending on the light of day and the weather. The same color is applied to the garage door to integrate it with the home. Creamy white trim helps the porch spring to the forefront and brings crisp definition to the windows, walls, and entry. A traditional dark green hue draws out the windows and the front door.

What's My Color Palette Quiz

The color of your house is a public statement of your personal self. Here's a fun way to nail down your style ... and thus your perfect paint job. Answer the following questions, then turn the page to read about what color palettes match your personality.

ABOVE AND RIGHT: Look to your favorite neighborhood, dream car, and wardrobe for color cues to outfit your home's exterior.

> **1. My friends say I am:** A) Reserved. B) Laid-back. C) Sentimental. D) Bold. E) Creative.

> **2. My closet holds:** A) Khakis and white shirts or blouses. B) Natural fibers in natural colors. C) Timeless, old-school fashions. D) Black and gray clothes with few embellishments. E) One-of-a-kind styles in a rainbow of colors.

> **3. My favorite CDs are:** A) Classical. B) Folk, Americana. C) Ballad-heavy. D) Pop. E) Every genre you can imagine.

> **4. My dream meal features:** A) Everyday American done just right. B) Free-range and organic foods, seasoned with herbs. C) Hand-me-down comfort-food recipes. D) The latest fusion fad. E) Spicy, exotic flavors.

> **5. My dream car is:** A) Practical and stylish with a great safety rating. B) A sporty hybrid. C) An antique roadster. D) The latest German model. E) A funky convertible.

> **6. My ideal home setting is in:** A) A neighborhood with two-story colonials and manicured lawns. B) The woods, by the water ... anywhere where nature rules. C) The country, surrounded by fields of wildflowers. D) An urban setting, with minimalist landscaping. E) Any area loaded with different home styles.

CURB APPEAL COMMENT: Shotgun Wedding?

First paint choices don't always work for paint jobs anymore than first dates work for people. Try a patch test—even sampling several of the same hues—before you cover the whole house.

> **Now tally the number of each letter you circled.** The dominant letter corresponds to the personality below.

A **Traditional:** On the conservative side, you like things nice, neat, and orderly, and that's exactly the statement you want to present to your neighborhood. Your classic sensibilities will make choosing your palette simple, as you clearly know what you do and don't like. One thing: Consider zesting up your makeover with a boldly painted front door. It's a small way to add style and punch without rocking the boat too much.

B **Nature-Lover:** You'd live in a modernized tree house if you could. But since that's not exactly feasible, take your cues from the things you clearly love—trees, plants, water, earth—and your house will present itself as a soothing oasis. Just make sure your home doesn't blend into its setting so much that your house is lost in the woods, so to speak. Instead, give your place a little pop, calling it out with crisply painted trim.

C **Romantic:** You think that a house has charm when the color fades, and the paint's gone all chippy. But thanks to the shabby chic trends of past years, there's a world of fresh color choices that will resonate with your soft tastes (see photo, *opposite*). And that predilection for peeling? Know it comes at a cost—lower resale values and higher repair costs down the road. So make a compromise: Tend to your home's exterior, then fill it with worn antiques—you'll have the best of the new and the old.

D **Modern:** Clean lines and sharp design really get you fired up. And while others may think mod means stark, you know it really means bold and innovative. So even if your house is traditionally styled, the monochromatic schemes you love will express your contemporary side. Enjoy your color combo options and continue to stay ahead of the curve, toying with surprise pairings that fuel you. One caveat: Don't get so absorbed in the latest trend you forget to work with your surroundings.

Artsy: You love anything that makes a creative statement and you collect the eclectic, whether that be furnishings or friends. Celebrate your one-of-a-kind spirit with an offbeat, funky color palette that invigorates you to the core. And as you sass up your homestead, keep in mind that the best artists reign themselves in a little, all to make their statements come through loud and clear.

HERE'S WHAT THEY DID

Although there was nothing exactly wrong with the Gillette's existing house color, there was nothing exactly *wow* about it either. Wife Aisha wanted to warm up the home's streetside facade, which didn't receive much sunlight. Husband Stephen said guests often had trouble finding their place—which is located on a monochromatic block of similar rowhouses. *Curb Appeal* designer Daniel Owens created a fix for both problems.

Owens traded in the house's French Country style for a Venetian paint job that looks as if it came straight out of Italy. The new palette, which involved replacing the gray taupe facade with a warm shade of terra-cotta, takes the home from wallflower rowhouse to sidewalk standout. To draw attention to the roofline, the coins—or cornerstones—that previously faded into the facade are now painted taupe. Owens repeated the taupe coloring of the cornerstones on the garage and service doors to lighten the entrance.

Further creating a welcoming facade to draw visitors in, Owens improved the garage lighting. He also lightened up the pavement leading into the garage by hiring a local artist to paint a faux-stone design on the hardscape. Other details complete the exterior overhaul in style—colorful mosaics mortared to the step risers add Italian detailing, custom-made iron tree guards bring an architectural element curbside, and verdigris-painted ironwork on the balcony, security gate, and facade details add curves to the overall exterior.

Photo Details >>>

1: Gold-leaf house numbers above the door are easy to spot.
2: The formerly single-tone step risers are mortared with colorful mosaics.
3: Faux stones hand-painted on the cement by a local artist create a custom look.
4: Dabbing the ironwork with verdigris paint (and wiping off all but the residue) softened the stark appearance.

Even if you're not ready for a major exterior overhaul, there's plenty to learn from the color and detail used on the Gillett's revamped rowhouse. Here's an overview of how they brought a little Italy home.

Before: A gray taupe facade that feels cold and dreary
After: A warm shade of terra-cotta that makes the house inviting while still complementing the nearby homes

Before: Single-toned steps and a dark, tunnel-like stairway

Before: Dull pavement leading into the garage
After: Faux stones hand-painted on the existing cement

After: Colorful mosaics mortared to the step risers to break up the monotony

Before: Dark, straight-laced ironwork
After: Curvy, verdigris-painted facade details

123

1 2
3 4

4

WELCOME HOME

Dive Into Divine Drives, Gorgeous Garages, and Perfect Paths

At the end of a long trip, whether the plane is touching down at the airport or you're driving into your neighborhood, you're bound to feel a sense of relief: You're almost home. In a perfect world, pulling into your driveway or walking the path from the street to your front door should inspire you and give you that same serene feeling—that of landing safely at home base— every day. If, however, your drive looks like a tired old airstrip and your walkway rivals a black-diamond hiking trail, a *Curb Appeal* makeover is likely in order. Lucky for you, this chapter is loaded with easy updates that won't take longer than a weekend. So roll up your sleeves and read on to make coming home a pleasure, not a pain.

Follow the Path to Success

Paths have a two-fold purpose: first, to lead guests from public areas, such as the street or drive, to the front door; and second, to provide a short tour of your front yard and its landscape.

Take a moment to analyze your walk. Is access obvious from a guest's standpoint? Does it offer top views that show off your front yard? Is it in good condition and safe overall? Whether it's time for a minor upgrade or a complete overhaul, start with these steps.

> **Plot a new course.** Pull out the site plan that you made in Chapter One—when it comes to placing paths, this overhead view is essential. Imagine you are laying out a stream (a path) and later, a river (the drive), as all

hardscapes should flow from end to end. Mark the "from" spot on the site plan to note the path entrance, then the "to" spot, the front door. As you draw potential routes, try following the curves of the land and wind around keeper plants, trees, and other elements. Don't meander too long—the goal, after all, is to get from point A to B, and you don't want to take away too much precious landscape space. If you get stuck, tour the neighborhood and look at your dream house tear sheets again. Seek out houses with similar terrain and mimic their choices. After you have an idea of what you'd like, put the garden hose (or a rope) to work, laying it on the ground to plot the path. Step back and study it from the curb, asking yourself if it feels right and is sensible. Walk the "path," judging the views, the width, and the length. Adjust until you hit on the best solution. When it's a go, mark the new route with stakes or landscape-safe marking spray paint.

Does Your Path Measure Up?

Experts agree on the following dimensions and details for a perfectly proportioned walkway:

Width: Between 3^1/$_2$ to 4^1/$_2$ feet wide

Landing: At 6- to 8-step intervals

Steps: From 5 to 7 inches high, 3^1/$_2$ to 4^1/$_2$ feet wide, and 2 to 2^1/$_2$ feet deep

Railings: Include for any set of stairs with more than 4 steps

OPPOSITE: A curvy sidewalk edged with brick spices up a gently curving route past the dry creek and decorative grasses to the front door.

CURB APPEAL COMMENT: arrive to Open arms

Pep up an existing squared-off walk or drive by widening the mouth of each entry with brick. Modify an upside-down V with curved, outstretched "arms" to give a welcoming, enveloping feel.

Universal Appeal Adding easy-access ramps and paths makes a house feel like home for those with restricted mobility. Boardwalk-style ramps are common solutions, but make sure they look like part of the house architecture (not a tacked-on appendage) and paint them in the house palette. Poured concrete and asphalt also work well, considering their smooth surfaces. Pavers can be another option, so long as they lie flush and seams don't make for a bumpy ride. In all cases, use landscaping to blend ramps into house entrances as seen from the curb. Here are key ramp dimensions:

- **Slope:** No more than a 1-to-12 ratio
- **Turning Radius at Landings:** At least 5×5 feet on ramps, and 5×6½ feet at doorways
- **Width:** 3½ to 4 feet
- **Handrails:** 32 inches high

> **Choose materials.** With your layout work behind you, it's time for the fun part—shopping. On the show, designers often take homeowners on field trips to local home improvement centers to check out the latest offerings for path and drive materials. It's a great idea, because that's one of the most efficient ways to see what's available locally—and at what cost. Try this in your hometown and explain your project to expert salespeople, who can give you needs-specific and regionally appropriate advice. If you're unsure about tackling the tasks yourself, ask a clerk if the project is a do-it-yourself one, or if you should hire a contractor. An alternative to shopping straightaway is exploring your surrounding community to see materials in context. While touring, if you see something that appeals to you, ask your neighbors how they felt about the performance and longevity of the products they used. Before you do either, though, review the chart on page 66 of the most popular materials offered today.

ABOVE: Stone stairs seamlessly blend a natural landscape with a rustic front entry framed by stone columns.

OPPOSITE: Use stepping stones to lead visitors to the front door or an outdoor seating area.

CURB APPEAL COMMENT: Watch Those Trees

When laying out a fixed material path, be wary of tree roots. Plan paths away from surface roots; otherwise, whatever you lay down will be pushed back up, leaving an uneven walk and cracks in its wake.

ABOVE: Loose stones such as pebbles or gravel create an easy-to-install front path. Pavers offer another option and look particularly organic when spaced so grass grows between the bricks.

Path Material Options

Asphalt Hot mixture of gravel, sand, and petroleum that cools into a smooth, hard surface. **Turn-ons:** Fares well in cold climates and is easy to repair. Looks less stark than plain gray concrete. Applying sealing layer refreshes the appearance and performance. **Turn-offs:** Can be dreary, seemingly industrial, and overbearing in color without proper layout, details, and landscaping. Professional installation required. Softens in heat and can thus be compromised in hot climates.

Boardwalk Series of planks laid out as decking and slightly raised from the ground. **Turn-ons:** Creates a beachy, pierlike feel. In top shape, makes a level path. Staggered with landings, can be a good solution to tough terrain. Inexpensive. **Turn-offs:** Less pricey materials weather roughly and require regular maintenance.

Brick Heat-fired clay composite in rectangular blocks. **Turn-ons:** Earthy colors give an organic feel. Modular shapes allow for a variety of patterns. Labeled as MW for moderate weather zones, and SW for severe weather zones. Great choice for novice do-it-yourselfers on a budget. **Turn-offs:** Not as durable as new alternatives, like pavers. Can grow slick and slippery with mild mildew growth. Can foster moss growth in cracks.

Cobbles Rough-hewn blocks of stone. **Turn-ons:** Old-world, classic style. Endures for centuries. Authentic stone, thus natural colors. **Turn-offs:** Expensive. Irregular surfaces make it slightly uneven. Not widely available and usually require professional installation.

Concrete Blend of sand, gravel, pebbles, and cement mortar that is mixed and then poured into frames where it dries smooth and solid. **Turn-ons:** Inexpensive, strong, durable. Multitude of stains, materials, stamping options create alternative finishes. Novice-to-moderate do-it-yourself friendly. **Turn-offs:** Cracks, stains, and ages. Can be too starkly pale if untreated.

Gravel, Pebbles, etc. Loose stones of varying size. **Turn-ons:** Huge selection of materials, colors, textures. Widely available, can be inexpensive, easy and quick to install. **Turn-offs:** Not the easiest to walk upon. Even with borders, material spills out of pathway and can be tracked into the house and street.

Flagstone Stone cut into large, flat pieces a few inches thick. **Turn-ons:** Variety of stones (slate, granite, marble, limestone, sandstone) offer wide range of looks. Large price range. Projects rank from easy, one-day affairs to the more involved. Classic look. **Turn-offs:** Slick when wet. If not fixed, can sink or move to make an uneven surface.

Natural Materials Mulch, crushed shells, etc. **Turn-ons:** Add an element of sound to the landscape (quiet padding or crunching). Super-simple to install. Organic look and feel. **Turn-offs:** Substance escapes the path (or drive) easily and thus requires replenishment.

Pavers Poured concrete blocks. **Turn-ons:** Modular and earthy with a hand-hewn feeling. Variety of shapes, sizes, and colors make for scores of patterns and looks. Stronger than brick. Mimic brick, tile, and stone in appearance. Widely available. **Turn-offs:** Moderately expensive.

Stepping Stones Flat stones placed in grass, loose pebbles, or other natural materials in lieu of a continuous surface. **Turn-ons:** Can look boldly artistic (poured concrete with tile mosaics) or subtle. No-brainer to install. Can be a temporary solution. **Turn-offs:** Usually camouflages path from street front. Doesn't necessarily facilitate easy passage.

CURB APPEAL COMMENT: Step Lightly

Is tough terrain a problem for your front path? Use a series of steps and landings to gently crisscross problem spots.

Devise a Dream Drive

Curb Appeal designers encounter it all the time: cookie-cutter neighborhoods where all the homes face the street at the same angle and driveways shoot straight from garage to curb without finesse. Tired of that monotony? Who's ready for one-of-a-kind parking?

If you can relate to that makeover itch, here's how to stand out from the crowd, whether that means repairing or altering your current drive, or learning how to install a new one.

> **Heal me! Repair and make amends.** If a redo isn't a reality for you, you have more options than simply restore and go. Tend to cracks, stains, and the like, and then consider your options. You can stain concrete, affix flagstones to many existing surfaces, work in brick or paver designs, or take a single swath of drive and convert it to treads. Need more room to move and park? Add stone, brick, or pavers to the sides of a drive to widen it with flair. Or maybe you want an entirely new parking spot—if so, tack on a pebbled side space.

> **Lay it out.** For those building new drives from scratch, ask what wasn't working in the old drive (color, performance, style, durability, layout) and then review your dream house tear sheets to create a wish list. Just as you did when laying out your front path, you'll want to use your site plan and around-the-house tools such as a rope and garden hoses to mock up the new drive route. Keep in mind that car doors should open without hindrance, and getting in and out of a car should be easy, not awkward.

TOP RIGHT: If your drive leads to a two-car garage, make certain it's 20 to 22 feet wide.

RIGHT: Determine whether your current drive is salvageable—you might be able to repair the existing surface rather than tear it up.

OPPOSITE: Stone pavers break up an otherwise boring expanse of driveway, connecting it with the surrounding landscaping.

CURB APPEAL COMMENT: Get Professional Help

When it comes to laying out a superior driveway, it doesn't hurt to hire a designer or contractor, as they specialize in problem-solving and tried-and-true solutions.

Sometimes handling the down and dirty parts of a *Curb Appeal* makeover—the repair and installation work—is easier than deciding on design. If planning stumps you, keep these two things in mind when determining layout style and colors for drives and paths.

Style: Formal Colonials and boxy modern homes work well with straight-lined paths and drives that emphasize their crisp bone structure. Similarly, cottages are made even cozier with winding walks and drives. But it's all a matter of what you want to play up or down. If you want to de-emphasize an austere look, for instance, incorporate curved paths and drives with circular parking courts; if you want to formalize a romantic dwelling, add direct paths and drives.

Color: Create a unified palette on your property and opt for materials in colors that complement your home, garage, and landscape. The best hardscapes blend into the environment.

The following standard dimensions are essential for laying out the ideal driveway.

- Construct 10 to 12 feet of drive width for one car or 20 to 22 feet for two.
- Tack on 2 feet of additional space for drives that double as paths.
- Create turnarounds 10 feet wide by 18 feet long with a radius of 16 feet.
- Substitute a drive with a parking court of 10-by-20-foot spaces per car.
- Allow drives to slope no more than $1^3/4$ inch per foot.
- Ensure water runoff with a slope away from the house of at least $1/4$ inch per foot; or build a drive with a slight crown (or crest) down the center to direct drainage to the sides.

> **Master materials.** Except boardwalks, the same materials used for front paths make good fodder for drives. Keep in mind, though, that the more durable types—such as concrete, brick, and stone—are more likely to withstand years of car weight and wear. If an expanse of any one of those still doesn't appeal, consider switching to a tread: two strips of solid stone, concrete, or other similar material with a contrasting material—groundcovers such as grass or dwarf mondo grass, pebbles, or rocks—running down the middle. Or you might opt for open pavers, which have empty middles that allow grass to sprout through. For ideas on updating one of the country's most common drive materials—concrete—turn to pages 74.

ABOVE: A curving gravel drive leads past a ranch-style home, ensuring passersby have plenty of clearance under the massive tree.

OPPOSITE: A black asphalt drive provides ample space for the homeowners and guests to park.

HOUSE RENDER REMINDER
Before you move on to the next chapter, add your new drive, path, and garage details to your rendering and site plan.

Go For a Great Garage

Ideally your garage passes as an extension of your house, one that houses another room, not just a carport. More than likely, though, you're dealing with a building that's little more than a glorified shed with expansive doors—and it's the first thing you notice from the curb.

If that's the case, your newfound mission is to make your garage look as much like a carriage house as possible. Say it aloud: carriage house. The words alone are charming. Follow the tips below to create your dream garage.

> **Tip One:** Update garage doors by adding windows. The style and size should complement doors and windows on the rest of the house.

> **Tip Two:** Replace garage doors with new ones that have gatelike details.

> **Tip Three:** Give the garage a fresh paint job, using the same overall color scheme as employed on the main house. Be sure to paint trim and interesting details too.

> **Tip Four:** Use hardware and lighting to dress up the utilitarian look. All add-ons should be a similar style to

RIGHT: Look for garage door styles that match the architecture of your home to enhance the overall design.

OPPOSITE: When it's outfitted with stylish doors and windows, you can play up a prominent garage.

those used on the front door, landing, and rest of the exterior.

> **Tip Five:** Add large rectangles made of trim to the garage doors, painting them the same color as trim elsewhere on the house. (Make sure add-ons don't interfere with opening and closing doors.)

> **Tip Six:** Flank garage doors with planters or topiaries, two on either side of a single-car garage, adding one in the middle in a two-car garage. Choose (or paint) containers the same color as the house trim.

Do It Yourself or Hire a Pro?

Several of the remodeling ideas in this chapter are novice friendly, but then there's that little business of learning (or admitting?) how much of a novice you are. To help you decide what to heap on your to-do list and what to pass off to a pro, read on:

If you can chop ice and ice a cake ... Then you can repair a crack in concrete.

If you can complete a jigsaw puzzle ... Then you can lay a brick sidewalk.

If you are a novice battling steep terrain ... Then hire a pro to design and implement your drive or pathways.

If you need to build a ramp with a rise to meet a front landing ... Then hire a pro for a consultation about a firm berm.

If you are intimidated by the thought of operating a jackhammer ... Then hire a pro to do your demolition work.

If you don't feel confident you can create a smooth slope for your drive ... Then hire a pro.

Curb Appeal Concrete Class

Concrete is one of the most popular materials used in American driveways for a reason: It's inexpensive, easy to install, and works in most climates and terrains. How's that for equal opportunism?

Yet many people who have concrete drives are troubled by the way concrete looks and wears or don't relish the thought of tacking the same old gray monolith to their unique homesteads. If you count yourself in either unhappy group, don't despair. Take the *Curb Appeal Concrete Class* to inject pizzazz into what you already have or zest up what you're about to lay down. Read on for the basics.

> **Repair.** If you plan to keep your concrete as is, or if you'll be altering it with superficial changes, repair work is most likely in order. Sweep or blow the surface clean, and hose off. After it dries, inspect your drive, noting mildewed spots, stains, and cracks. Mend each in the following prescribed manner.

- **Mildew:** Power wash or remove with a mixture of one part bleach to three parts water.
- **New oil spill:** Soak up with cat litter.
- **Old stains:** Power wash with bleach solution. Stubborn stains may require store-bought concrete stain remover. Use sealant to guard against problems.
- **Cracks:** Power wash. Fill small cracks with masonry caulk or concrete compound. For large cracks, use a chisel to hammer off crumbling concrete and widen opening until edges are sound. Cut down to the layer of earth below the concrete. Line bottom with smooth layer of stones or sand. Add concrete compound and smooth with trowel. Once dry, apply concrete sealer over entire surface of drive.

> **Redo.** If you like the shape, scale, and layout of your concrete drive but you want a different appearance, clean and repair it, but skip the sealant stage. Instead, try staining it. Stains come in scores of different shades, and their mottled look helps conceal repairs and other irregularities. If a cover-up is more your speed, consider creating a faux limestone coat or laying down flagstone directly atop the old surface.

> **Remove.** So you're completely over your concrete drive? Be prepared to work off some aggression. Brawny types will need chisels and sledgehammers. Others fare best renting jackhammers from a local home improvement store (or hiring out the work). Follow jackhammer directions and, wearing your goggles, start about 6 inches from the edge. With both sledge- and jackhammers, your goal is to break the surface into pieces small enough for you to handle and remove.

RIGHT: With proper planning, laying a new concrete drive can go off without a hitch, as in this *Curb Appeal* episode.

OPPOSITE: To keep your concrete drive looking good, power wash regularly and repair cracks as soon as they appear.

Visit HGTV.com/homestylequiz to see what type of architecture suits you best.

CURB APPEAL COMMENT: WATCH THE WEATHER

Concrete is best for moderate to warm climates, as it requires more sealing and repair work in snow-prone areas. Asphalt may be the better choice for extremely cold areas.

BEFORE

AFTER

HERE'S WHAT THEY DID

Frank Pelzer is a coastal kind of guy. He grew up in the waterfront town of Charleston, South Carolina, and now lives in a fishing village on the West Coast. While he loves his cozy cottage with its view of the bay, he wished the place looked a little less California contemporary and a little more Cape Cod.

Thanks to landscape specialist Daniel Owens and home expert Kem Theilig, the hardscape, plantings, and house received some makeover magic.

To update Frank's straight-shot driveway and ho-hum garage, the designers replaced the pale gray concrete drive with a dark-stained concrete that complements the new charcoal-hue house shingles. Widening the drive meant the old, ill-planned path from the curb to the ground-level door was obsolete. This left room for a new retaining wall of textured landscape blocks, which winds around a front-yard plant bed. Because of its faux detailing, the garage's new single-unit door appears to be two separate doors, which gives the garage a small-scale, carriage-house character in keeping with the seaside cottage look.

Before, visitors had a tough time finding their way to the second-story front door. To remedy this, the designers replaced Mexican tile-covered walkways with concrete pavers that lend the appearance of cobblestone. A new arbor at the street-side steps clearly announces the entrance to the front path, which leads to the newly remodeled deck and front door entrance.

Photo Details >>>

1: A new retaining wall of textured landscape blocks winds around planting beds and softens the yard's curves.
2: The new garage door is framed by lights that further its carriage-house character.
3: A compass in the bowl of the birdbath is painted in colors the complement the home's exterior.
4: Concrete pavers add an old-world cobblestone feel to the walkways.

If you're struggling to plot out and refinish your drive or paths, take these tips for building a winning, warm welcome way.

Before: Plain, untreated concrete in a pale shade of gray
After: Dark-stained concrete to blend the drive with the environment

Before: An off-to-the-side, tough-to-spot front entrance on the deck

After: Deck stairs reoriented to the street and tied to the curb with a small, round patio and path for a straightforward entrance

Before: An easy-to-miss arbor that looks like an out-of-place afterthought

After: An arbor that replicates a Nantucket design and clearly announces the front path entrance

Before: A huge expanse of gray garage
After: A single-unit door that appears to be two doors thanks to faux detailing

1 2
3 4

5

FRAME YOUR YARD

Add Fab Fences, Wonderful Walls, Hot Hedges, and Grand Gates

Imagine these scenes for a moment: An open field edged with a line of tall trees; a rolling countryside bordered by distant mountains; a beach hugged by a series of tall cliffs. In each case, the landscapes in the foreground are made more distinct by the elements that frame them in the background.

Just what does that have to do with your front yard? Everything. At this point in your *Curb Appeal* makeover, it's time to play border patrol and determine what fences, walls, hedges, gates, and the like you'll employ to best frame your own landscape. Whether you need these boundaries for aesthetics, practicalities, or a combination of the two, learn how defining your space can be as simple as digging holes for a hedge or stacking stones for a short wall.

Know What You Want

Study your front yard from the curb. While contemplating what borders to add and where to place them, focus on function and style. Now is the time to determine which borders will make your wants and needs a reality.

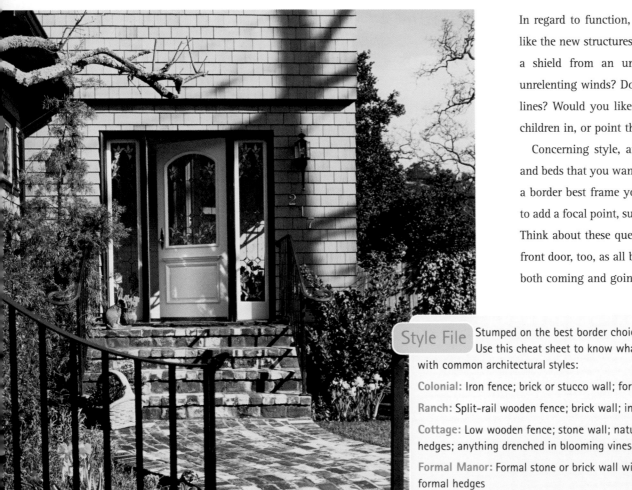

In regard to function, ask yourself what purpose you'd like the new structures to fulfill. Do you need privacy or a shield from an unpleasant view, traffic noise, or unrelenting winds? Do you need to mark your property lines? Would you like to keep animals out or pets and children in, or point the way to your front door?

Concerning style, are there existing or future plants and beds that you want to highlight with edging? Would a border best frame your green space? Are you looking to add a focal point, such as a whimsically shaped arbor? Think about these questions while looking out from the front door, too, as all borders should serve the landscape both coming and going.

Style File Stumped on the best border choice for your home? Use this cheat sheet to know what typically works with common architectural styles:

Colonial: Iron fence; brick or stucco wall; formal hedges

Ranch: Split-rail wooden fence; brick wall; informal hedges

Cottage: Low wooden fence; stone wall; natural-shape hedges; anything drenched in blooming vines

Formal Manor: Formal stone or brick wall with iron details; formal hedges

Bungalow: Natural-looking stone wall; natural-shape hedges

Mediterranean: Stucco wall with metal accents; formal or informal hedges and topiaries

CURB APPEAL COMMENT: Sidestep The Problem

Dealing with building a border on rough or steep terrain? Use natural materials such as stone or hedges to follow the land's natural lines.

Fence Me In

The old cliché about good fences making good neighbors is right on the money: A little boundary goes a long way to give those of us living side-by-side some breathing room to call our own.

Fences are one of the most ubiquitous borders because they offer such a vast price range and encompass a variety of styles. Done well, fences can also be one of the friendliest-looking ways to delineate what's yours and what's your neighbor's. And for those into immediate gratification, fences go up faster than any other option. Read on to see if a fence is in your future.

> **Put it in place.** Fences range from waist-high affairs to towering numbers. Consider the functions you aim to achieve and mock up a faux fence to see whether the staged version accomplishes those goals. First sketch potential fences on your house rendering. When you've settled on placement, plant temporary stakes appropriately and run orange plastic fencing between each. Adjust the height and location of this faux fence until you settle on what looks best. Once you've nailed it down—figuratively speaking, at this point—include the fence on your house rendering and your site plan, then start shopping for materials.

Do It Yourself or Hire a Pro?

Are you sure that border patrol is your line of duty? Take a look at these hints to see what's in your jurisdiction and what's worth passing off to the pros:

If you can stack a set of kids' plastic building blocks ... Then you can make a low wall.

If you can dig a hole ... Then you can plant a simple hedge.

If you can paint an interior wall ... Then you can paint your own fence.

If you need a major retaining wall ... Then hire a pro to build a safe and effective one.

If your border covers rough or excessively steep terrain ... Then hire a pro with experience building on similar landscapes.

If your soil is either impervious or too wet ... Then hire a fence builder or landscaper to incorporate work-around solutions.

RIGHT: A simple white-painted picket fence is easy to build and maintain, and it provides a romantic backdrop for plantings on both sides.

OPPOSITE: To ensure a seamless transition from curb to house, match your fence style and color to that of your house.

CURB APPEAL COMMENT: **Tune Up Time**

Keeping your border as is? Tend to the hardware, and repair any wall cracks, wood rot, iron rust, or sickly hedges.

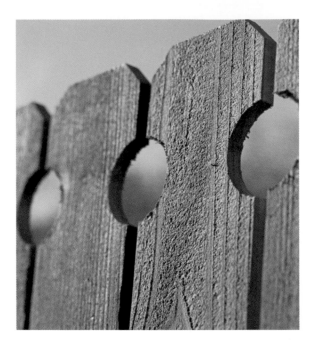

> **Build with the best.** The mix of materials available for fencing is as elaborate or as simple as your creativity and your budget allow. Here's an overview of what's most readily available.

Wood: Widely available, wood can be manipulated into a variety of looks, and can be purchased natural, stained, or painted. Go affordable with found limbs and inexpensive lumber, or spend more with fine woods such as cedar and redwood. Good for moderately skilled do-it-yourselfers, wood does require regular maintenance—it must be stained annually and repainted every three to five years. Remember that wooden post bases must be treated or affixed to cement anchors to offset underground weathering from pests and wetness. Posthole depth depends on zones and frost permeation. *Types and styles*: bamboo, picket, stockade, basketweave, lattice, louvered, board-and-batten, post and rail, split rail, alternating boards

Metal: A safe, long-lasting alternative to wood, metal requires little to no upkeep and is widely available and inexpensive. Keep in mind, however, that it's best installed by professionals. Iron fencing may rust and, as such, requires periodic stripping and painting. It can

look cold and uninviting if not softened with landscaping. *Types and styles*: chain link (available in black, green, or unpainted silver); wrought iron (can be decorative, with spiked tips for safety); artistic (copper or steel pipes)

Alternatives: Vinyl, wire mesh, and rigging offer solutions that traditional methods can't. Vinyl is a long-lasting option that requires less upkeep than other materials. Best framed with wood, wire mesh allows unobstructed views. Consider using rigging for a railing if you're working with metal or wood for a bold statement. Depending on what material you choose, prices may be higher than with typical fencing options, and professional installation might be required.

ABOVE: If you plan to build your own fence, consider using wood. Keep in mind, however, that this affordable option requires regular maintenance.

LEFT: Soften a simple wrought-iron fence by grouping colorful potted plants near its base.

CURB APPEAL COMMENT: Size Down

If a fence's only fault is its height, cut a few feet off the top and add new post toppers, rather than replacing it entirely.

Work a Little Wall Magic

For thousands of years, walls have stood as the ultimate territory marker, radiating a sense of permanency and connection to the past. Emulate the classic sensibilities and steadfastness of the world's wonderful walls by creating your own style statement.

Fine choices for safety and privacy, walls can also be super practical, acting as retainers to prevent erosion and helping a terraced garden climb a steep front yard. To open yourself up to the possibilities offered by walls, take stock of the suggestions that follow.

Show Your Soft Side No matter the style or building materials, any broad, impenetrable expanse of wall gains visual appeal when softened. To that end, try these tips to add a little warmth:

Hang plants from various points on both public and private sides.

Top walls with planters to add year-round or seasonal color.

Train vines to grow across walls.

Foster mossy growth by spreading a blend of equal parts water and buttermilk (or yogurt) across brick or stone walls.

Mount a wall fountain or other yard art to break up blah spaces.

Paint walls in colors that echo the house palette.

Add murals or trompe l'oeil scenes on stucco or wood panels.

Mix and match materials, using a wall-and-fence combo.

Stack bricks or pavers in pierced latticed patterns to allow light and breezes to break through.

> Size it up: Don't get carried away with grandiosity. Depending on what you want to achieve, walls can be effective whether they are knee-high or up to 8 feet tall— a standard maximum height. Think of the low variety as the means to define an area (plant beds, a path, or an outdoor room) and save tall walls for privacy and security purposes, when possible. To determine placement, try the same method mentioned for staking out a fence line, or simply place a row of rocks or bricks in along the intended location (great for lower borders). Conventional wisdom says that walls 4 feet and shorter are safe bets for do-it-yourselfers to construct; beyond that, you're best served heading to the pros.

RIGHT: A solid concrete wall decked out with plantings ensures privacy and stands the test of time.

OPPOSITE: A grand wall matches the stucco color of the house it surrounds, beckoning passersby to enter.

Get more ideas for gates, fences, arbors and more at HGTV.com/hardscaping.

CURB APPEAL COMMENT: Demolish to Polish

Use safety goggles and a sledgehammer to tear down old walls. Recycle bricks or stones for paths, low walls elsewhere, or to edge plant beds and paths.

Good Cents Sense

- Finish a low base wall with an inset fence, rather than building an 8-foot-tall, solid wall.
- Substitute kits for handcrafted gates, arbors, or fencing.
- Leave wall or fence entrances open, instead of gating them closed.
- Use hedges in place of other building materials.
- Stain—don't paint—wood fences and walls.
- Top fence posts with wood caps, not copper or stone.
- Opt for faux cast stone over true cobbles.

> **Choose your building blocks.** What you use to build your wall and how it is designed is part of the personal statement your house and yard make to the public. Opt for Fort Knox styling and even if your walled-off area is the friendliest, coziest space in your ZIP code, no one but you will ever know. Instead, play nice neighbor and stick with styles that suit your area and that are consistent with your overall redesign. Use this list of materials for further guidance.

Brick: Available in myriad colors and tones, brick is a moderately priced choice, depending on the variety you choose. Styles stacked latticelike deliver an open look with the same sound barrier effect as a solid wall. Know that all brick walls require mortar.

Wood: Generally speaking a wood fence allows views and light to show through, while a wooden wall is solid. Be conservative with wall placement—use them on side yards to block an undesirable view, to close in an outdoor room, or to create privacy in small spaces. If overused, wood walls can quickly create a claustrophobic feel.

Stucco: Vinyl or textured cement plaster spread over a concrete, cinder block, or brick base, stucco has an earthy appearance. Best used with houses that are either fully stucco (such as some Mediterranean or Southwestern styles), or those with stucco foundations, installation is best left to professionals. Choose the same paint shades used on your home.

Stone: The beauty of stone walls is that they don't have to be mortared together, as long as they are stacked soundly, rise from a base just below the ground surface, and thin slightly at the top. Used as low borders, high security walls, and retaining walls, stone looks natural and blends into nearly all landscapes, allows for seepage of water and material expansion, and is easily repaired.

Alternatives: Manufacturers always find a way to improve upon yesterday's offerings, or even nature's best. In the wall world, that means that a variety of precast materials mimic the best of the old with today's enhanced performance. Concrete pavers, faux stones, and landscape blocks are all available for walls.

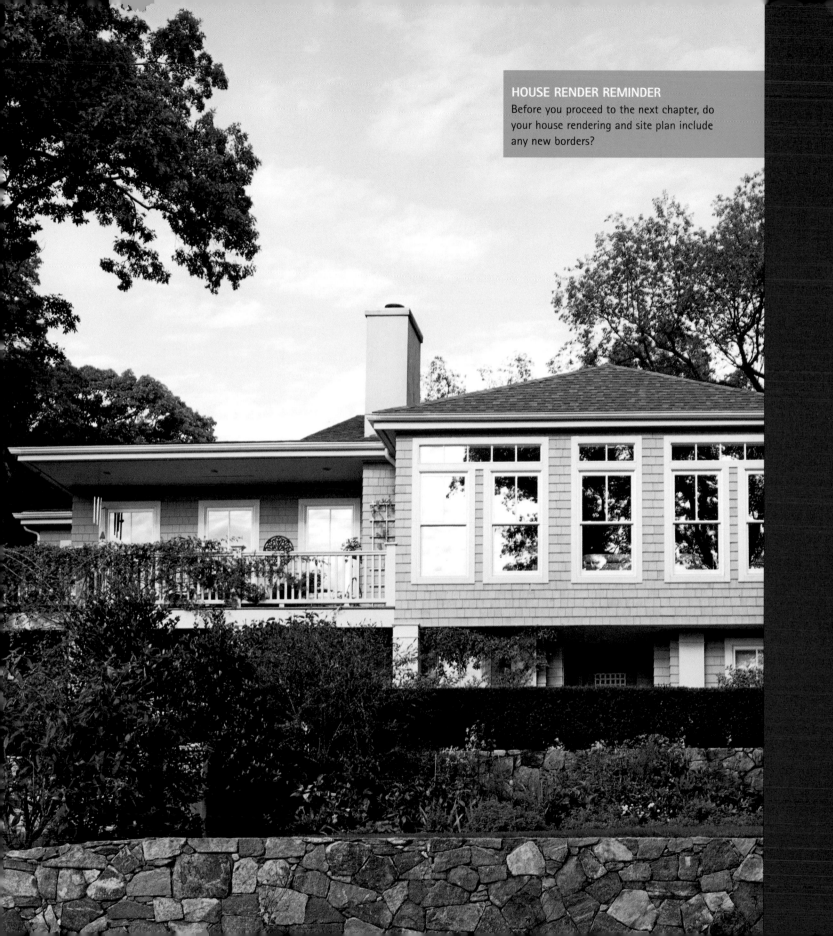

HOUSE RENDER REMINDER
Before you proceed to the next chapter, do
your house rendering and site plan include
any new borders?

Consider Gates, Hedges, and Arbors

Look beyond the basics of fences and walls to find a world of options waiting to play. Envision a hedge for privacy and security, add a gate to greet guests in style, or place an arbor for a front-yard focal point to up curb appeal exponentially.

OPPOSITE: A pretty white gate surrounded by potted plants and trees beckons guests to enter.

> **Go for gorgeous gates.** If a front door is the welcoming committee to your house, your front gate is the greeter to your yard. Given its prominent role, take your time to choose a gate that extends the welcome you wish to share. Do you want to invite visitors in, or present a more formal face? Choose a style, materials, color, and hardware to reinforce your message. Keep these dos in mind.

• **Do** break up monotonous stretches of fencing or walls with a gate.

• **Do** erect a freestanding gate in the opening of a mature hedgerow.

• **Do** guide traffic to paths with gates.

• **Do** buy or build gates 4 feet wide for paths and 12 feet wide for drives.

• **Do** invest in sound latches and hardware.

• **Do** allow gates to open fully without obstruction or hindrance.

• **Do** place hinges and latches out of children's reach.

• **Do** erect a freestanding, decorative gate to mark a transition from one part of a yard to another.

• **Do** search local salvage yards for vintage gates.

• **Do** ensure that gates are operable for those with restricted movement.

Perfect Hedge Picks

Your best options for formal hedges are boxwood, juniper, holly, privet, and roses. Try an azalea, camellia, hydrangea, lilac, potentilla, pussy willow, viburnum, rhododendron, rose of sharon, or spirea for a more informal option.

> **Have haute hedges.** If you want the same effect as a fence or wall but crave something more organic, less permanent, and potentially less expensive, hedges make a great substitution. Incredibly versatile, they can be as short as your calf or as tall as your house. Formal hedges and uniform shrub varieties clipped into sharply defined shapes can be laid out in patterns that range from mazes to monograms. Less formal hedges can look as though they naturally grew in just the right spot. Often planted in staggered clusters, such hedges include various shrub varieties, all pruned to look barely tamed. Both styles are novice-friendly: If you can dig a hole, you can plant a row. On the downside, hedges can take years to properly fill out; they require tending (watering and trimming); and if a large, mature shrub dies out, the gap creates a hole that's expensive to plug.

OPPOSITE AND RIGHT: Place an arbor over a key entry point to direct traffic to the front door. Climbing vines add an element of color.

Climb the Walls

Looking for just the right vine or plant to cover your wall, fence, or arbor? Study plant tags to see if they are suited for your location (shade, soil, and zone) and the integrity of your border structure (wood, stone, brick, or chain link). Know that evergreens (ivy and fig, for example) tend to look terrific year-round, while others show their best face during warm months. Here are some great options:

- Bean vines
- Black-eyed Susan vines
- Bleeding heart
- Bougainvillea
- Clematis
- Coral vine
- Creeping fig
- Honeysuckle
- Ivy
- Jasmine
- Morning glory
- Passion flower
- Purple parachute
- Roses
- Trumpet vines
- Wisteria

> **Add an arbor.** Like gates, arbors mark passageways from one space to another. But these freestanding trellised frames have freedom to roam. Place an arbor anywhere you want to add a focal spot, whether it's at the foot of a path to direct visitors to your front door or at the beginning of a secret side garden. You also can use an arbor in a fence composition (in lieu of an elaborate gate) to save money without compromising style. Though arbors are ideal for weekend-project people, keep in mind these caveats:

- Bury support posts as deep as half an arbor's height or anchor them in concrete.
- Use treated or otherwise impervious materials, as wooden arbors are highly susceptible to rot.
- Paint or stain wooden or metal arbors to protect them from the elements.
- Plant vines to grow over your arbor.
- Buy an arbor kit or preassembled model to save time and energy. You'll pay more, but the cost of convenience might be worth it.
- Install a vinyl arbor if low maintenance is the name of your game.
- Choose a design and construction that withstands conditions your arbor will encounter—strong winds and vines, for example.

BEFORE

AFTER

HERE'S WHAT THEY DID

When it came to advertising his talents, Mark Christiansen worked way below the radar. Although he's a top-notch builder who updated the inside of his bungalow to showplace stature, and he's a car buff who transforms relics into hot rods, the outside of the single dad's Craftsman home divulged nothing of his ample skills. While the house was as sound as they come, the exterior paint scheme was subpar, the yard a scrappy mess of rocks and rubble, and the drive a two-rut dirt track. Factor in a 6-year-old son who needed a safe play space, and the Christiansen cottage desperately needed a makeover.

That's where designer Yvonne Lane Wonder and landscape planner Cody Shrey came in. They knew the solution lay in creating a system of borders to define the lot, but the lack of landscaping had to be addressed first. After laying out a new, curving drive, a front walk, and an alternate side path, the basic overall structure of the remaining green space came alive, which allowed the designers to plot out new fences and gates. The team added a new picket fence to the front yard and repaired an old one that spanned the back and side yards—both of which complement the earthy colors of the house. To direct traffic to the front door, they built a pergola at the street-side entrance and added plantings to both sides of the walkway. Now, Mark's young son has a fabulous yard in which to play, and Mark finally has an exterior worthy of what his home holds inside.

Photo Details >>>

1: A new porch swing provides a perch for Mark and his son.
2: The curving fence with its staggered picket heights offsets the house's horizontal lines.
3: Street-side visitors are greeted by the new pergola and fence, which are stained to complement the house.
4: Pebbles fill the spaces between the concrete squares of the side path.

If you're starting from scratch too or if you're ready to wipe your slate clean and add borders, learn from Mark's front yard makeover.

Before: Strict lines and no contrast
After: A fence that gently follows the curving arc of the front drive

Before: Nothing delineating the lot from the street sidewalk

After: A new fence and plantings on both sides of the railings

Before: An inaccessible front door
After: A pergola trellis at the entrance of the front path to direct traffic

Before: A shoddy backyard and side fence with loose and rotten boards
After: An instant, easy upgrade—replacement boards, a power washing, and new paint

1 2
3 4

6

ROOM TO RELAX

Bring Indoor Comfort Outdoors

There's no finer way to soak in the great outdoors than by sitting in the middle of it. After all, why not take in the view from a comfy chair or vintage rocker on a shaded front porch? Where better to keep tabs on the neighborhood than from a discreetly placed garden bench? Where else would you savor a fresh-from-the-grill summer dinner than at an outdoor dining table? And where better for kids to romp and play tag than on a grassy expanse on the safe side of a picket fence? An outdoor room can be as elaborate as your dreams or as modest as your budget with little sacrifice and a whole lot of payoff. Bring the comforts of indoor living outdoors so you can reap the benefits of your new *Curb Appeal* landscape. After all, why go to all this trouble improving the front of your home if you're only going to enjoy it when you pull in the driveway or walk up to the front door?

Max Out What You've Got

The endgame of a *Curb Appeal* makeover is to create a space in harmony with your house and lifestyle, one that's user-friendly and takes advantage of all that your front yard has to offer. Add an outdoor room to capitalize on what makes your space unique.

Safe Harbor If you have the room and a little bit of privacy, bring these typically indoor activities outdoors. Use this list to ensure your outdoor room has the proper amenities:

Sleeping Space: A quiet, comfy place to lay one's head; screening from the street; overhead shelter a plus

Cooking Space: A grilling area or cooking pit, preferably with a chimney; counterlike space a bonus

Meditating Space: Peace and quiet; a sheltered area that soothes the senses; shielded from the street

Gardening Space: A potting shed or cupboardlike piece of furniture to house tools and necessities

Bathing Space: Privacy screens; outdoor showerhead or tub with plumbing; recommended for side yards or high-walled front yards

Working Space: Desk or table and comfortable chair; level ground in quiet space; electrical outlets nearby

Whether you're faced with tiny quarters or a sprawling expanse, create fresh-air rooms that work to your advantage by following these steps.

> **Choose your location.** The best outdoor spaces offer level or nearly level ground with a total or partial view of the yard. Walk your lot as they do on the show, searching for a suitable location, one that has easy access to paths or is set on easily traversable terrain. You'll know you've landed in the right place when you want to stop to survey your surroundings. Even if you don't have a porch and don't plan to add one, a front yard location can work well. Another option is along the side of your house, facing the street. Hedges and fences that border the "room" or the front property line define the space and can help to block street noise.

TOP LEFT: An ideal sleepin[g] relaxing space is easy to c[ome] by when stringing a hamm[ock] from a side yard fence or a[ ] pair of sturdy trees.

BOTTOM LEFT: Privacy is [key] when building an outdoor [ ] shower. Be sure to use [ ] materials that complement [the] style of your home's exteri[or].

ABOVE: Outfit a porch with a daybed and chairs to create a comfy nook for reading or resting.

CURB APPEAL COMMENT: Check Your Weight

Make sure your balcony or deck can withstand any added weight your makeover may add. A formal once-over by a local building inspector is the best way to avoid accidents.

BELOW: For a cozy getaway, all
you need are the basics. Here,
chairs surround a tree stump table.

OPPOSITE: A path leads visitors
past structures such as vine-
covered trellises and arbors in this
pretty side yard.

> **Lay the groundwork.** Preparing an outdoor room means starting at ground level. If you're dealing with virgin land, first create an even surface and tend to drainage issues. When that's settled, determine the flooring: consider spreading pebbles, fine-grain gravels, or mulch; planting a bare-foot friendly groundcover; laying bricks, pavers, or flagstones; or building a low deck. Concrete flooring also offers several options.

> **Add borders.** Using Chapter Five for guidance, consider the borders you'll use to delineate your outdoor room. The edging you choose (whether it's a low, mossy brick wall; a primly trimmed waist-high hedge; or a tall, vine-drenched partition) acts as the walls of your room, giving it definition and emphasizing the space as a focal point or downplaying it with a discreet screen.

Add a Little Structure to Your Yard

When your house and landscape demand a formally designed outdoor space, add a little structure to the mix. Review these garden structures to find one that best suits your situation:

Arbor: Framework of beams, posts, and trellises that combine to form open side walls and roof. Meant for visual interest, gateways, shading seating, and more. Can be gatelike (without the door) and often covered in vines.

Garden Shed: Spacious sheds can be adapted to create an outdoor room. Alter or remove doors and windows to make the structure more inviting.

Gazebo: Carousel-looking structure with open sides and level floor.

Pergola: Similar to an arbor, pergolas are usually more hefty and less ornate versions of arbors.

Trellis: Latticed frames that support climbing plants and vines, trellises can be used to create outdoor walls.

> **Sketch your space.** After settling on the location, decide if the space is a nook, a room, or perhaps an extension of an existing structure (a porch, patio, or courtyard). Is it sized for a little bench or large enough for a table and chairs? What is the ideal setup, given its size and terrain constraints? Sketch your ideal room onto your site plan.

Floor Yourself

Rugs—whether they're weatherproof or not—are best used under protected overhangs such as porches and porticoes to shield them from inclement weather. Look for rugs that clearly state their weatherproof qualities. Your best bets are propylenes and other synthetics that can be hosed down for cleaning. If you can't pass up a natural fiber rug, spray it with waterproofing sealant to protect it from damage. Although bamboo and grass varieties look best outdoors, they don't hold up to wet conditions.

> **Decorate.** An empty room is a blank slate begging for decoration. Jump in, but remember to work in conjunction with your house style. Start with seating—decide how many people you can accommodate without cramping or cluttering the space, and determine where to place chairs and benches. Next, consider tables. Can you fit a bistro table, a large picnic table, or a side table? Add cushions, pillows, tablecloths, and other linens. Finally, incorporate artwork, including pieces such as fountains and outdoor sculptures. As always, keep to the same color palette as your house exterior: The goal is a uniform look that complements the entire scene as viewed from the curb.

ABOVE: The chipped white-painted wood of this weathered table and chairs creates a romantic spot for dining on the porch.

OPPOSITE: Decorated to serve as a gardener's haven and a resting spot, this cozy porch invites visitors to sit a spell.

Fair- or Foul-Weather Furniture

Outdoor furniture has to survive the same unrelenting weather your hardily constructed roof does. That's a tall order, but thankfully, there are plenty of options up to the task. Here are some materials that fare well, fair weather or foul:

Aluminum: Rustproof and thus a popular choice, most painted aluminum furniture comes with its own protective coating. Use car wax to boost the weatherproofing properties.

Cast Iron and Steel: Heavy enough to withstand strong winds, these metals will rust if untreated. Tend to problem spots as they appear: Sand, prime, and cover with rust-resistant outdoor paint.

Painted Wood: Allow it to weather for a chipped, romantic look, or spray with clear weatherproofing outdoor enamel and paint. Wash with a brush and soapy water as needed.

Resin: Apply car wax to avoid staining.

Synthetic Wicker: Resistant to mildew, cracking, and rot, it's nearly identical to natural wicker. Wash with a brush and soapy water to remove dirt and dust. (Note: Keep natural wicker in sheltered locations, cleaning similarly, and coat with linseed oil to avoid cracking and splitting.

Teak: Ages naturally, fading from caramel to gray. Any treatment other than teak oil compromises the wood, so leave untended unless professionally directed.

Browse dozens of designer outdoor spaces at HGTV.com/outdoorrooms.

CURB APPEAL COMMENT: Be Color Correct

Coordinate your porch, patio, and deck furniture and fabrics with your exterior house colors.

Order Off This Roomy Menu

Stumped over what to make of a cleared outdoor space? Set up a chair and ask yourself what you want to capitalize on. Is it the view? The hideaway factor? The chance to dine alfresco? One must for all rooms is a place to sit—beyond that, it's up to you.

Make a wish list, then look at this sampler platter of popular options.

> **Perfect porches.** Porches range from covered landings and shaded nooks under porticoes to languorous affairs that wrap all the way around a house.

No matter the size, each has two things in common: a sheltered covering and a view of the yard and street. Consider porch space as socializing-central and dress it accordingly with comfortable seating (rockers, sofas, lounge chairs, gliders, swings) and side tables. If it's a primo napping spot, add a hammock. And if you're aiming for privacy, hang billowing curtains or shades. Suspend plants from the eaves, place container pots along the stairs, and mount window boxes where possible for seasonal color.

Porch must-have: A dreamy view.

Fabulous Outdoor Fabrics

Pillows, cushions, and linens are the extras that transform an outdoor room into a comfy getaway. Because not all fabrics and finishings are created equal, here's how to make sure yours can stand being left out in the cold—or worse—from time to time:

Acrylic: Practically mildew- and fade-resistant, acrylic fabrics are usually coated with weather- and stain-resistant finishes. They are produced in a range of colors and patterns that mimic the look and feel of natural fibers. Clean with a gentle soap. When mildewed, wipe with 1/2-cup nonchlorine bleach in 5 gallons of water.

Cotton: Canvas, twills, and duck cloth are tough fabrics that handle rough wear and tear. But even they are no match for misty mornings and the occasional summer shower. Stick to using natural fibers on decorative throw pillows you can pull in overnight or during stormy weather. Weatherproof with outdoor fabric and waterproofing sprays and reapply after each wash-and-dry cycle. Fading is inevitable, but part of cotton's charm.

Spun Polyester: Unlike other fabrics, spun polyester is by nature water-repellant. Wipe spills and clean dirt off with soapy water; no bleaching or weatherproofing needed.

Clasps and Closures: Opt for nylon zippers. Unlike their metal counterparts, they won't rust. Choose weatherproof nickel-covered snaps.

RIGHT: Sheer curtains hang from a porch, providing privacy and shade when closed.

CURB APPEAL COMMENT: Let It Grow

If your landing or porch is too shallow to accommodate a room, expand it beyond its original overhang.

HOUSE RENDER REMINDER
Add any new garden structures and outdoor rooms to your site plan and rendering.

> **Sit-a-spell spaces.** Sit-a-spell spaces take the social aspects of a porch and move the party elsewhere: under open skies, in a little side yard, or just off the front door on an extended landing, for example. These places beg for twosomes, whether that means a couple catching up at the end of the day, best friends chatting over a glass of wine, or a parent and child stargazing well after bedtime. Such conversations require cozy seating for smaller parties—think a pair of Adirondack chairs, a cushy bench for two, or a set of teak loungers and you have the right idea. Add a focal point near this space. A water garden with fish, a birdbath, a portable fire pit, or a gazing ball collection warms up the chat du jour.

Sit-a-spell must-have: A fantastic focal point.

> **Playful playrooms.** Nothing beats playing outside, so imagine your yard as the ultimate game ground. Do you need an area for boccie, badminton, or croquet? Do little ones need room to wheel about on tricycles? In each case, borders are essential, as they prevent groundcovers such as sand and pebbles from escaping, and they restrict children in playpen fashion. Consider low borders that double as seating, perhaps a brick or stone wall. And make sure that groundcover suits potential activities: grassy stretches for barefoot hide-and-seek, smooth cement for riding scooters on sandy alleys for tossing horseshoes.

Playroom must-have: Great groundcovers.

ABOVE: Potted plants nestle up to a sandy boccie court that's ready for play.

LEFT: A corner courtyard with a petite pond is the perfect spot for a table and chairs.

CURB APPEAL COMMENT: Recycle

Look in salvage and secondhand shops for outdoor furniture. A little wood glue in the joints and a paint job can breathe new life into oldies but goodies.

Do It Yourself or Hire a Pro?

How extreme your room addition is determines whether you're best off hiring help or going at it alone. Here are some guides to help you make up your mind:

If you can move a sofa ... Then you can place a new bench in your front yard.

If you found the perfect furniture for inside your house ... Then you can find your dream furniture for outside your house.

If you can hang a picture ... Then you can hang a hammock.

If you can paint your front door ... Then you can paint and protect outdoor furniture.

If you can build model toys ... Then you can put together outdoor furniture, and maybe even kit railings too.

If you can level ground and pour concrete ... Then you can make a new patio.

If you want anything higher than ground-level decking ... Then hire a pro for a consultation, if not more.

If you have massive drainage or terrain issues ... Then hire a pro to build your room base.

If you don't have time, tools, or know-how to build an outdoor room ... Then hire a pro, and tackle the plants and decor yourself.

> **Cozy courtyards.** The most private and secluded of outdoor rooms, courtyards are enclosed spaces shielded from public view by tall plantings, walls, or other substantial partitions. Perfect as outdoor dining rooms, they house large tables and chairs and lounge furniture for kicking back between meals. Decorate this space as you would an interior room. Include outdoor art and sculpture, water and container gardens, and even outdoor rugs.

Courtyard must-have: Divine dining table and chairs.

ABOVE: A stone wall and iron fence combine with a carved fountain, sculptures, and potted plants for an intimate retreat.

CURB APPEAL COMMENT: Play Musical Chairs

Have a bench in the backyard going unused? Bring it into the front yard to create a social space.

BEFORE

AFTER

HERE'S WHAT THEY DID

Before the Ikeda household bustled with an active family of four, husband Mike and wife Alisa would head to the nearby hills for a spa getaway when they craved a break. Since those opportunities are few and far between these days, the pair wanted to bring that element of escape closer to home. When *Curb Appeal* designer Will Wick took the pair to a local spa for "research," they all agreed its style—a West Coast, Tuscan villa hybrid—was worth re-creating back at the homestead.

That's how the Ikedas came to have their very own suburban oasis. By converting their front porch into an outdoor room and putting in the right landscaping, they scored a soothing sanctuary steps away from the front door.

Large redwood column covers anchor the porch with a rich, earthy element. Drab, gray-blue shutters were replaced with custom-made shutters that introduce a classic, weathered copper finish to the porch space. New wood doors with a gorgeous, warm honey stain and metal hardware exude contemporary chic style.

The highlight of the redesign is, of course, the porch itself. Teak chairs and a cafe table framed by weather-resistant curtains create an intimate gathering space. Candles popped into sand-filled, amber-color martini glasses set the seating area aglow at twilight. The view from the porch includes the newly tamed front yard, which is an emerald carpet of fresh sod. To complete the aura of a spalike retreat, fruit trees and lavender offer their sensual, soothing scents when the Ikedas linger on the porch.

Photo Details >>>

1: Curtains frame a cozy seating area with cushioned, all-weather teak chairs.
2: Olive trees in copper-finish containers and low-growing plantings flank the stairs.
3: New lanterns, address numbers, and a garage door give the space a cohesive style.
4: An elegant flagstone porch floor and front path replaced the plain cement.

If you're ready for a relaxing retreat in your front yard, take cues from the Ikeda's spa-worthy *Curb Appeal* overhaul.

Before: Dinky, out-of-scale columns
After: Large redwood column covers beef up the old pillars

Before: Overgrown lemon trees and shrubs
After: Low-growing foundation plantings

and olive trees in copper-finish containers

Before: Steps as the only seating option
After: All-weather teak chairs and a cafe table

Before: Too-bright afternoon sun

After: Weather-resistant curtains protect seating area

Before: Old, etched glass doors
After: New wooden doors with a warm honey stain and stately metal hardware

1 2
3 4

MASTER LANDSCAPING

Follow These Tips for a Fantastic Front Yard

Ask a child to sketch their dream home and sure enough, there's a house, a towering tree, an emerald lawn, and a few colorful flowers scattered about. Why the green extras? Because even kids know that landscaping makes a house a home. Yes, indeed, leave it to Mother Nature to soften the edges of the most austere architecture and make the sweetest cottage more endearing. As seen from the curb, a dream combo of trees, shrubs, flower beds, and groundcovers flow out from any front door like a red-carpet welcome. To give your address that same open-arm feeling, keep reading for step-by-step advice that will land you in every kid's front yard fantasy.

Survey the Site

What's the first thing that *Curb Appeal* designers and homeowners do after introducing themselves? They take a hike—to evaluate the house and property, of course. Do likewise and check out your landscaping as seen from the trenches.

The Perfect Plant Picker Quiz Not sure about what trees, shrubs, and plants to plug into your site plan? Use this list of questions to determine what will work in the allotted space, and match your answers to the specimen specifications labels on plants sold at garden centers. If you get stumped, talk to a sales clerk, call a county extension agent, or ask a local garden club for suggestions.

- Is the planting area in full sun or full shade?
- If it's part sun or shade, how many hours a day does it get of each?
- What is the soil condition (clay, sandy, dry, wet)?
- What is the soil's balance? (It's either alkaline, high pH; or acidic, low pH. Buy an inexpensive pH testing kit at a local nursery or garden center, or take a soil sample to a local extension agent.)
- How wet is the area? What's the drainage like?
- Do you need plants that prevent erosion?
- Are you a diligent gardener or do you need low-maintenance plants?
- In the case of flowers, do you want perennials or annuals?
- In the case of shrubs and trees, do you want evergreens or deciduous?
- What size plant do you need?
- What size, shape, and color plant would complement your house?
- What existing plants will occupy the same bed or area?
- Is there masonry, pavement, or other hardscapes nearby?
- What is your plant zone?

Look at the existing flora, terrain, drainage and erosion issues, and shady versus sunny spots. Make a list of your lot's assets and problems, then a dream list of wished-for elements. For a little local inspiration, explore your neighborhood and note favorite homes with front-yard conditions and topography similar to your own. When you have a feel for what you want in your space, determine what will stay, what will be removed, and what will be added. Draw keeper trees, plants, and beds—mark them as circles and bed-shape bubbles—on your site plan. (As you follow this chapter, plug any new elements into the plan as well.)

ABOVE: Instead of fighting a sloped front yard, work with it by using retaining walls and tiered planting areas.

OPPOSITE: When surveying your yard, you might decide to keep elements such as a stone bench, while replacing flowers or bushes.

CURB APPEAL COMMENT: all in Due Time

There's a saying that the first year a newly planted landscape sleeps, the next year it creeps, and the third year it leaps. Patience is key to realize a truly comprehensive landscape plan.

> **Landscaping problems and solutions.** Sometimes a landscaping problem needs to be solved before you can plant your yard. Other problems can be worked out by planting the right specimen. Here's a little insight into the most common issues homeowners face, and ways to solve potential problems.

ABOVE: To level out acidic soil's balance, add compost or fertilizer.

BELOW: A concrete retaining wall combined with plantings prevents erosion.

Acidic Soil

• **Gardening Solution:** Level out the soil's pH balance by adding sulfur or fertilizer with ammonia; or go organic and add compost, sawdust, or peat moss.

• **Plant Solution:** Choose acid-loving plants: azaleas, camellias, rhododendrons, hollies, ferns, pines, heather, bleeding heart, and lupine.

Akaline Soil

• **Garden Solution:** Balance the pH with lime.

• **Plant Solution:** Go for alkaline-loving plants, such as privet, spirea, boxwood, some maples, cherry trees, yew, sunflowers, and peonies.

Dry Soil

• **Irrigation Solution:** Use soaker or drip hoses to water conservatively.

• **Plant Solution:** Use drought-resistant plantings, such as native grasses, low-water groundcovers, and herbs such as sage, rosemary, thyme, and lavender.

Erosion

• **Landscape Solution:** Use terraces and retention walls to interrupt water runoff. Cover the area with porous landscape fabric or mulch until plantings grow.

• **Plant Solution:** Opt for native grasses, shrubs, trees, and groundcovers, as they require less watering than imported varieties. Use plants with various depths of root systems to boost soil retention and ease water runoff.

Sloped Terrain

• **Landscape Solution:** Level slight slopes by adding fill dirt and perhaps a retaining wall; build terraces to create beds along steeper slopes; add a waterfall.

• **Plant Solution:** Cover the bank with a low-maintenance groundcover: Virginia creeper, honeysuckle, certain roses, ice plants, ivy, and clematis.

Wet Soil

• **Drainage Solution:** Clear the area and build a French drain, then plant as needed.

• **Plant Solution:** Install plants that thrive in boggy conditions: ferns, irises, marsh marigolds, and certain types of hostas.

CURB APPEAL COMMENT: Guide Traffic

Use plantings to help direct traffic: Line paths that lead to your front entry with beds and plant turf alternatives in areas where you want to discourage walking.

Treasure Trees

Trees dominate a landscape, so it's best to plot them first. While they add romance to any scene—imagine the wind rustling through the leaves, a swing hanging down from a stout limb, hidden birds chattering in the canopy—trees also offer loads of practicalities.

In hot months, trees provide shade for your home (cutting up to $270 off your seasonal air-conditioning bill), guard against erosion, act as wind and sound screens, and increase your privacy. To choose the best tree for your yard, consider the following:

> **Placement.** A backyard oak big enough to rise over a roofline makes a house appear larger from the front. But plant that same tree just before the front door and the house is obscured, as are views out. Lesson learned?

Think about the maximum size your tree will reach and place it accordingly. Stick to the ends and corners of your house or deep in the yard to play it safe, being mindful of roof overhangs and power lines that could interfere with a full-grown specimen. Likewise, avoid root-induced cracks in sidewalks, drives, and foundations by planting trees with roots that run deep rather than those with roots that spread shallow.

ABOVE: A variety of deciduous and evergreen trees, bushes, and vines cover and surround this tiny home.

LEFT: This mature tree, as well as the trees surrounding it, lends shade to the front yard.

OPPOSITE: A stone path leads to the entrance of a home tucked in a forest of fall foliage.

CURB APPEAL COMMENT: Be Gone!

Call the power company to trim or remove existing trees that interfere with power lines.

Acer palmatum (Japanese maple) DECIDUOUS. **Characteristics:** Green to red star-shape leaves that turn deep burgundy in fall. **Growing Conditions:** 15'–20' tall. Full sun to part shade. Slightly acidic soil. Zones 6–9.

Cercis canadensis (redbud) DECIDUOUS. **Characteristics:** Purple berrylike spring blossoms. Heart-shape leaves that turn yellow in fall. **Growing Conditions:** To 35' tall. Shade tolerant. Indiscriminant soil. Zones 4–8.

Gingko biloba (gingko or maidenhair) DECIDUOUS. **Characteristics:** Fan-like leaves that turn gold in fall. **Growing Conditions:** 50'–80' tall. Full sun. Moist but not wet, slightly acidic soil. Zones 5–10.

Malus (crab apple) DECIDUOUS. **Characteristics:** Spring blooms, summer fruit. Weeping shape. **Growing Conditions:** 15'–25' tall, depending on variety. Full to partial sun. Acidic soil. Zones 3–8.

Prunus (stone fruit tree) DECIDUOUS. **Characteristics:** Apricot-, cherry-, peach-, or plum-bearing. Spring flowers, summer fruit. Varied fall colors. **Growing Conditions:** To 25' tall. Depends on type of tree. Zones 4–10.

Pseudotsuga menziesii (Douglas fir) EVERGREEN. **Characteristics:** Spiraling clumps of blue-green needles; bright green new growth in spring. Long cones and fragrant foliage. Dwarf varieties good for hedges. **Growing Conditions:** 80'–100' tall. Sun to partial shade. Acidic, moist but not wet soil. Zones 5–9.

Pyrus calleryana (Bradford pear) DECIDUOUS. **Characteristics:** White flowers in spring, bright red leaves in fall. Oval leaves. Pyramid silhouette. **Growing Conditions:** 25'–35' tall. Full sun. Moist but not wet acidic to neutral soil. Zones 5–9.

Quercus (oak) DECIDUOUS/EVERGREEN. **Characteristics:** Leaves depend on type, but vary from oval evergreens to full deciduous kinds. **Growing Conditions:** Height ranges based on type, from 30'–100' tall. Conditions vary due to type, and span the full range of acidic to sandy soil, full sun to full shade. Zones 4–9.

Tilia cordata, T. x eucholora (linden) DECIDUOUS. **Characteristics:** Dark green, heart-shape leaves with white early summer flowers. Pyramid silhouette. **Growing Conditions:** 35'–70' tall. Full to part sun. Neutral to slightly alkaline soil. Zones 4–9.

> **Shape.** Choose trees by shape, too, as mature canopies form into silhouettes that can complement the lines of your house. For example, round and weeping trees (weeping willows) add curves to a boxy house and make large dwellings appear cozier; just as tall, conical trees (cedars) add height to low-lying homes.

> **Variety.** Decide on deciduous (seasonally leaf shedding) or evergreen (permanently leaf- or needle-bearing) varieties. For further help narrowing down your selection, check out the plant picker sidebar on page 114.

Zone In

The United States Department of Agriculture designates 10 plant hardiness zones across the country. Low numbered zones represent cool climates, and numbers closer to 10 represent hot ones. See page 189 to determine your zone. Match your plant choices to your zone for happy, healthy, and hardy specimens.

ABOVE: Be mindful of roof over-hangs and power lines when selecting a spot for your trees.

OPPOSITE LEFT: The spiraling clumps of needles that grow on a Douglas fir are fragrant.

OPPOSITE RIGHT: A Japanese maple stands to one side of a driveway. The star-shaped leaves turn a dark burgundy in the fall.

Select Shrubs

Shrubs have many trunks, while trees sprout up from one central trunk. That variation aside, unchecked shrubs can grow to tree heights, so plant them judiciously and trim them often unless giant-status is your goal.

Pick, plot, and prune shrubs—regardless of their height—for personality and function.

> **Go formal.** Trim shrubs into distinct shapes for topiaries, or plant them in mazes and other patterns to give any stretch of land a formal feel.

> **Build a border.** Enlist shrubs as the ultimate green border. Hedges (see Chapter Five) screen out unwanted views, offer subtle privacy, and outline the edges of paths, property lines, and more.

Do It Yourself or Hire a Pro?

Green thumb or not, sometimes piecing together a new front yard can be a puzzle. For advice on when to charge ahead on your own or when it's time to call in a crew, keep reading:

If you can wield a nail clipper ... Then you can prune a shrub with garden shears.

If you can dig a hole ... Then you can plant any plant or build a French drain.

If you can stack building blocks, pot a plant, and fill a jar of water ... Then you can build a container water garden.

If you can spread a sheet on a bed ... Then you can prevent erosion with landscape fabric.

If you can buy clothes that suit your shape, coloration, and the occasion ... Then you can pick the right plants for your front yard.

If you don't have the tools (chains, saws, tow hitch) to remove a stubborn tree, shrub, or stump ... Then hire a removal service.

If envisioning an overall plan for your front yard stumps you ... Then hire a designer to map out a plan, give you a timeline for installation, and recommend what is DIY or professional territory based on your situation.

If you want to install a major feature (waterfalls, terraces, significant retaining walls) and have no experience ... Then hire a contractor to do the dirty work.

TOP RIGHT: For a formal garden, trim shrubs into distinctive shapes.

TOP LEFT: An ornamental grass border offers a casual, easy-maintenance option.

OPPOSITE: A plethora of bushes and plantings grow up a sloped front yard.

> **Act natural.** Plant shrubs in clusters, and prune them into loose, natural forms to create islands that break up expansive spaces.

> **Add balance.** Create a seamless transition between the height of a towering tree and a ground-level flower bed by adding midsized shrubs.

TOP: A curved border contains yew, hostas, impatiens, hydrangea, and quercifolia.

MIDDLE: Striped grass and yellow barberry will add a burst of sunny color to your beds.

BOTTOM: A boxwood hedge works to define a grass walkway or block views of a side yard from the street.

Shrubs

Berberis thunbergii (barberry) **Characteristics:** Dense with small, shiny leaves that turn to bright red in fall. Thorn-bearing with small red berries in winter. **Growing Conditions:** 3'–6' tall. Partial to full sun. Average to sandy soil. Drought-tolerant. Zones 3–8.

Cotoneaster (deciduous cotoneaster) **Characteristics:** Spreading branches with dark leaves. Small white flowers in spring; red berries in fall. **Growing Conditions:** To 2' tall. Full sun, well-drained soil. Zones 6–10.

Potentilla fruticosa (cinquefoil) **Characteristics:** Gray-green leaves in summer, yellow in fall. Buttercup-like flowers in summer. **Growing Conditions:** To 4' tall. Full sun, well-drained soil, moderate summers. Drought-safe and cold hardy. Zones 2–9.

Syringa meyeri (dwarf Korean lilac) **Characteristics:** Fragrant pink and purple flower clusters in early spring. **Growing Conditions:** To 5' tall. Full sun, moist, humus-rich soil. Zones 3–7.

Buxus microphylla (boxwood) **Characteristics:** Compact version of the popular evergreen shrub. Tightly packed, small, glossy leaves. Small flowers in spring. **Growing Conditions:** To 3' tall. Full sun, moist, nutrient-rich soil. Zones 6–9.

Chamaecyparis (false cypress) **Characteristics:** Graceful, layered branches with lacelike greenery infused with golden hues. **Growing Conditions:** Dwarf: 6' tall or less. Morning sun, afternoon shade. Moist, humus-rich soil. Zones 5–11.

Ilex (holly, inkberry) **Characteristics:** Tough, glossy leaves with thorned edges. Red berries in winter. **Growing Conditions:** Dwarf: 4' tall or less. Traditional English: 20' tall. Full sun to partial shade. Prefers acidic, moist soil. Zones 5–9.

Taxus (yew) **Characteristics:** Dark green curved needles 1"–2" long. Tufted branches. Some varieties produce small red berries. **Growing Conditions:** 3'–15' tall depending on variety. Full sun to shade. Moist, well-drained soil. Cool, moderate climate best. Zones 2–7.

Ligustrum (privet) **Characteristics:** Glossy, small leaves with clusters of white flowers and black berries. Good for hedges. Evergreen in South. **Growing Conditions:** 9'–15' tall. Sun to partial shade. Drought tolerant. Zones 4–9.

CURB APPEAL COMMENT: Buy the Whole Package

Make sure you like a plant's shape, limbs, leaves, and coloration, aside from any blossoms it may have. You'll likely see the flowers one season, and the rest of the plant for the remaining part of the year.

Flow in Foundation Plantings

Dust ruffles and kick pleats hide legs, conceal storage space, and connect furniture to the floor. Foundation plantings work similarly. Running around the house, they flare out like a skirt ruffle to camouflage foundations and any prominently placed utilities.

RIGHT: Taller plants—such as tiny trees and shrubs—look best when planted nearest the foundation, so they don't dwarf smaller plants.

BELOW: A variety of plantings situated in beds, pots, and window boxes defines a front entry.

OPPOSITE: A series of stone paths and walls defines and contains the foundation plantings on this steeply sloped lot.

As you piece together the recipe for your foundation planting, consider these five main ingredients: a tree on one corner; a series of shrubs along the front of the house; filler flowers in the seams; a groundcover over any bare earth; and a low-lying border (planted or hardscaped) between the planting and the lawn. Ideally, there should be a stair-stepping effect from taller to lower elements—the shortest being in the foreground. Otherwise bear these Do's in mind:

- **Do** choose plant varieties that you can maintain.
- **Do** allow room to grow. While compact plantings of hefty-size starter shrubs may look better in the short run, mature plants can soon overtake the space, the windows, and the house itself if not trimmed regularly.
- **Do** plant on the outer side of the roof's drip line, and away from downspout runoff.
- **Do** consider alternative plantings. If space doesn't allow a four-tier foundation planting—as with curbside homes—train a climbing vine (ivy or creeping fig) to grow over the foundation instead.

Make Your Beds

Beds are islandlike groupings of flowers and plants that break up sprawling spaces and transition between man-made hardscapes, structures, and nature. Beds are great spots to add a burst of seasonal color, and are thus favorites for any quickie makeover.

To add a bed to your yard, first choose the location, then place a garden hose on the site, shaping it to form the bed's exact outline. Trace the final parameters with flour, lime, or landscape-safe marking spray paint. If you can form a moist fistful of the soil into a ball, you're good to go. Otherwise, if the soil is too dry or too wet, add organic material such as leaf or pine bark compost, water accordingly, and repeat until the soil passes the fist test. Beyond that, follow these steps to prep and plant:

- Dig down along the entire border to make the edge.
- Turn up (or till) the earth about a foot deep throughout the bed.
- Remove rocks, roots, and other debris.
- Add additional soil to level gentle slopes.
- Add any necessary amendments, such as mulch, lime, and fertilizer.

LEFT: Use a stone border to contain flower beds. Add elements such as a birdhouse for decorative effect.

RIGHT: Planting flower beds can be as easy as fertilizing, digging, and placing plants in the ground.

ABOVE: Set plants on a bed while they're still in their containers to determine ideal placement.

In small front yards, stick to a simple color palette of greens and one shade of blooms to amplify the space.

- Mix in amendments by turning up the earth once again.
- Spot plants into their proper locations by placing them on the bed while still in their containers. Move containers around until you settle on the best positions.
- Mark plant spots with flour, lime, or landscape-safe marking spray paint.
- Dig holes according to the size of the plants going in the bed—two times as wide as the width of the root ball, and deep enough so root ball tops are at surface soil level.
- Gently place plants into holes, and add backfill to the halfway point, tamping soil down gently to set it in place. Water, then finish filling with soil, tamp down again, and water once more.

First-Rate Flowers

Hemerocallis hybrids (daylilly) PERENNIAL. **Characteristics:** Long, grassy-base leaves, bountiful lilylike blooms throughout summer. **Growing Conditions:** To 4' tall. Full sun or partial shade. Mild to neutral pH soil. Moist soil. Zones 3–9.

Hosta (hosta) PERENNIAL. **Characteristics:** Low, broad leaves vary in color, variegation, and texture. Some types have flowered spikes in summer to fall. **Growing Conditions:** To 3' tall. Shade. Low-water. Mild to neutral pH soil. Zones 4–9.

Dicentra spectabilis (bleeding-heart) PERENNIAL. **Characteristics:** Heart-shape pink spring flowers. **Growing Conditions:** To 3' tall. Prefers shade. Neutral to slightly acidic, moist soil. Zones 4–9.

Paeonia (peony) PERENNIAL. **Characteristics:** Large, fragrant, and fluffy flower heads in spring. **Growing Conditions:** To 4' tall. Full sun. Moist, slightly acidic soil. Zones 3–9.

Pelargonium (geranium) ANNUAL. **Characteristics:** Clustered blooms of red, pink, or white throughout summer. **Growing Conditions:** To 2' tall. Full sun. Drought-tolerant. Neutral to mild pH levels. Zones 3–8.

Petunia x hybrida (petunia) ANNUAL. **Characteristics:** Vine-like and leafy, offers a huge variety of wide-brimmed bugle blooms in many colors and sizes. **Growing Conditions:** To 1½' tall. Full sun to partial shade. Moderate watering. Neutral pH level. Zones 3–9.

Salvia splendens (salvia) ANNUAL. **Characteristics:** White, pink, rose, and purple. **Growing Conditions:** To 3' tall. Full sun. Average soil and water needs. Zones universal.

Narcissus (daffodil) BULB. **Characteristics:** Bright to pale yellow bugled flowers with ruffled edges. **Growing Conditions:** 6"–20" depending on variety. Sun or partial shade. Average soil and water needs. Zones 3–8.

Iris (iris) BULB. **Characteristics:** Large, broad leaves at base, delicate but showy blooms in a rainbow of colors. **Growing Conditions:** 6"–50" depending on variety. Sun or light shade. Average soil and water needs. Zones 3–8.

ABOVE LEFT: Flower beds add bursts of color throughout a yard.

ABOVE RIGHT: Plant pink salvia in a bed with a colorful mix of perennials and annuals.

Browse dozens of designer outdoor spaces at HGTV.com/outdoorrooms.

:8:4:5:

CURB APPEAL COMMENT: Get Edgy

Use bricks, pavers, fencing, or plastic runners to edge any bed, lawn, or path for definition and a crisp look.

Cover It Up With Lawns and Groundcover

Turf grass and creeping vines (or other ground-hugging plants that propagate) fill in the blank stretches of a yard in stellar fashion. For those who can't choose between a thick, healthy lawn or richly textured groundcover, here's a little decision-making help.

landscapers don't have time to gamble, so they opt for sod to repair sickly grass spots and create instant carpets in a flash.

To lay sod in your yard, clear the land of existing groundcover and grass, then prep the soil as you would for a plant bed. Rake across the top to create an ideal surface for new roots. Unfurl the sod rolls so they spread across (not down) any slope, staggering the seams from row to row. Press down along all seam edges, and roll over the sod with a lawn roller (available to rent from garden centers). Water thoroughly and often over the next three weeks while the new grass takes root, and wait up to one month to mow.

Whether you cover your front yard with green, fertile lawn or a different sort of filler, remember that this part of your yard should complement the trees, shrubs, and plantings you've already selected.

> **Lawns.** If you envision an emerald yard as the welcome mat to your home, a sea of turf grass is the way to go. While seeding grass can be less expensive than sod, the results are slow to show, and your hard work can wash away with the first downpour. *Curb Appeal*

CURB APPEAL COMMENT: MASTER MOW FLOW

Lay out your turf with mowing in mind. Grassy swaths should be wide enough for a mower to pass through, and slopes should be gentle, not overly steep.

All lawns are not created equal—use this guide to make certain you're choosing the right grass for your part of the country:

Bahiagrass: Does well in hot, sandy coastal areas with little maintenance. Region: National coastline.

Bermudagrass: Warm-weather and drought-tolerant grass with a long green season. Looks best with routine watering schedule. Region: National, best on West Coast, in South, and in the mild Midwest.

Buffalograss: Native grass that doesn't require mowing. Prefers sun, and turns honey-color during cold months. Region: Central Prairie states.

Fescue: Drought and shade tolerant. Region: National.

Kentucky Bluegrass: Prefers cool summers and full sun. Needs regular watering. Region: National except the deep South.

Perennial Ryegrass: Needs sun and moderate temperature. Fares best when watered regularly; does well in Southern winters. Region: National.

St. Augustinegrass: The coarsest of turf grasses, weathers full sun, and humid, warm weather well. Suffers frost poorly. Region: coastal South.

Tall Fescue: Drought-tolerant, cool-season grass. Grows well in full sun or partial shade. Region: National.

Zoysiagrass: Warm-season grass that fares best in hotter climes. Turns brown during cold months and greens again when it warms. Region: Central states.

> **Groundcovers.** If mowing a lawn is one of the least appealing tasks for you to tackle during your off-hours; if you prefer people stay on paths and walks; and if you've never had any luck growing grass, a groundcover is a low-maintenance alternative to turf. Great filler for beds, and ideal for steep slopes where grass cutting is out of the question, groundcovers offer a broad span of colors, textures, and personalities. Consider this handful of favorites.

- Flowering: Vinca, flowering thyme.
- Sun-loving: Juniper, creeping thyme, Asian jasmine, creeping sedum.
- Dark green: English ivy, pachysandra, dwarf mondo grass, liriope.
- Light greens: Ajuga, moss, bugleweed.

ABOVE: Vinca, with its petite purple flowers, is one example of a flowering groundcover.

LEFT: Pachysandra borders a slim brick walkway.

ABOVE: Even with the absence of a lawn, a front yard filled with groundcover and plantings looks green and inviting.

CURB APPEAL COMMENT: add Sprinkles on Top

For a cozy cottage lawn, choose a no-mow turf and sprinkle flower seeds on top to dot the lawn with tiny blooms.

Plant Portable Pots

Colorfully planted container pots are the easiest way to add seasonal color to porches, porticoes, landings, and patios. They're a portable, low-maintenance, low-commitment way to garden for novice and experienced gardeners.

Even better? You can shop for materials in the afternoon, and be done planting long before dinner guests arrive. Here's how to make a showstopping container garden of your own.

> **Choose the right pot.** Unglazed terra cotta pots absorb water and can crack when the temperature fluctuates, so opt for glazed varieties or bring unfinished clay containers indoors during cold weather. Otherwise, concrete, metal, plastic, wood, fiberglass blends, and vinyl make good alternatives. Regardless of material, ideal models have drainage openings in the bottom. If not, insert a container liner (or smaller pot) with drainage holes into the showy outer pot. Set the innermost container on a sturdy, level brick to allow excess water to run out—the larger pot acts as a catch basin. Choose containers large enough to allow for growth, and dig planting holes equal to root balls.

> **Dress up a plain or old container.** One *Curb Appeal* episode featured terracotta pots wrapped in rope for a dockside line spool effect. Follow suit and paint your pots with stripes, glue on mosaic tiles, or add stenciled patterns that work with the color palette and style of your newly made-over house.

THIS PAGE: Choose glazed or painted varieties of clay containers, or consider planting in wooden boxes instead of pots.

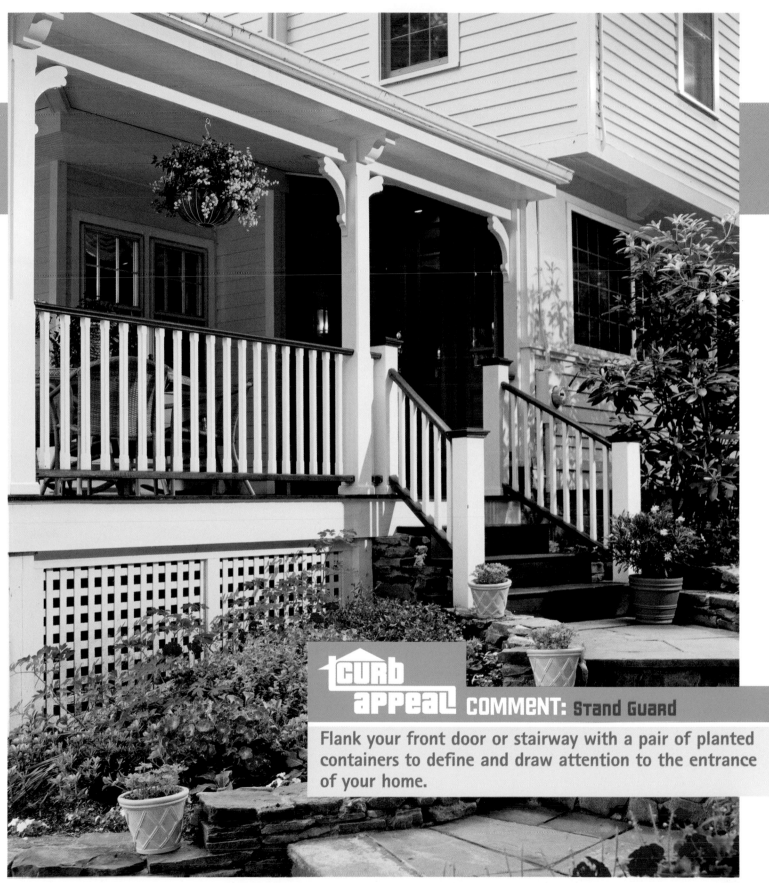

CURB APPEAL COMMENT: Stand Guard

Flank your front door or stairway with a pair of planted containers to define and draw attention to the entrance of your home.

> **Place it perfectly.** Window boxes obviously are meant for windows, but they do just as well set on an outdoor mantle, or suspended from porch and balcony rails. Round pots and square planters work best grouped in odd numbers of varying sizes, placed in corners and tucked into alcoves. For a casual look, place pots intermittently along stairs; for a formal look, place them in symmetrical pairs.

> **Pick the perfect plant mix.** Choose your plants in trios: first a spiky and tall one; next, a smaller and bushy specimen; and last, a trailing variety. Make sure their specs (sun, water, shade) suit where you'll place the pot, and that the colors complement each other, the house, and the container. Take your container to a nursery or garden center, and drop in sample plants to settle on the right combo.

> **Layer up.** Buy enriched container soil, or mix potting soil with sphagnum moss, perlite, garden loam, fertilizer, and moisture retention products available at garden stores. Plant square or rectangular containers (like planters and window boxes) in a staggered stair pattern of rows, shortest in front, tallest in back. With round pots, place the tallest sample in the center, then encircle it with medium-size plants, followed by the trailers.

ABOVE LEFT: The perfect planting combination includes something tall and spiky; a smaller, bushy plant; and a trailing specimen.

RIGHT: Window boxes work in more than just windows. Suspend one from a porch rail.

Watch videos on how to create a portable garden at HGTV.com/containergarden.

CURB APPEAL COMMENT: Go Faux

Containers and planters covered with metal-based finishes age with the same patina as true metals and cost less. Some are even painted in shades that instantly mimic the rusted or verdigris look.

Play With Themed Gardens

Themed gardens are a terrific way to determine your plant choices and layout style—particularly if your home is a distinct architectural type, if you have a definite love for a particular environment, or if freestyle landscape design overwhelms you.

Not sure where to begin? Take a look at the styles below to find one that matches your personality and your home's distinct style.

> **Ecletic.** Make your space stand out with boldly colored plants, a mix of textures and shapes, and garden art. For a harmonious result, complement (or tastefully contrast) plants to house colors and stick with the layout principles in this chapter.

> **Formal.** Use topiaries, primly trimmed hedges, containers, and planters amid pea gravel paths and masonry and stone walks for a low-maintenance, formal feel.

> **House Style.** Take a cue from your architecture: olive and lemon trees with rosemary for an Italianate villa; desert succulents and grasses for a Southwestern stucco home; and climbing roses, a wildflower "lawn," and flowering shrubs for a shingled Cape Cod cottage, for example.

> **Modern.** Use a mix of strictly edged beds in geometric shapes, metal-finish or concrete planters and containers, and firs. Soften the look subtly with a water garden or fountain.

> **Native.** Plant specimens that are distinct to your area: a tropical garden in coastal climates, a desert Xeriscape in the Southwest, a woodland escape in mountainous regions, for instance.

> **Romantic.** Prune trees and shrubs naturally, and plant weeping trees, flowering bushes, climbing vines, and groundcovers that send their scents wafting through the air. Aim for a secret garden look.

> **Traditional.** Follow the plant "recipes" in this chapter (ingredients: trees, shrubs, groundcover, flowers, and plants) and choose specimens based on local offerings and neighborhood favorites for a middle-of-the-road, traditional mix.

CURB APPEAL COMMENT: Size Matters

If you can, buy larger, more mature specimens when shopping for your makeover plants to get a head start on filling in your space. Smaller potted samples save a few dollars, but they take that much longer to grow in.

BEFORE

AFTER

HERE'S WHAT THEY DID

Feng shui expert Lilian Ng knows how to use ancient Chinese design philosophies to transform her clients' homes into oases that just plain feel good. But when it came to her own house and its feel-good factor, the curb appeal quotient was way out of whack. So fellow feng shui enthusiast and show designer Daniel Owens teamed up with Lilian to make her urban retreat into a harmonious spot swathed in positive energy.

To others who live with concrete front yards and past-their-prime architectural trappings, Lillian's problems were common: Too much hardscape, not enough greenery, choppy path and drive layouts, and silly exterior details did nothing to create an inviting home.

The existing pale yellow house color was fine, but there was nothing in the foreground to offset or complement it. Color balancing is a grounding principal of feng shui design, so the first step was to create an environment in which the gaze flows from one visual component to the other. Now, newly planted red flowers represent fire; green topiaries and groundcover represent nature; black fixtures represent water; brown pavers represent earth; and the white trim and trellises represent metal, all vital feng shui elements.

With no true property borders, the lot seemed sandwiched between two other homes. To remedy this, tiny-but-true gardens on either side of the front entry, a new plant bed along the property line, and vine-covered trellises on either side of the lot abide by feng shui's 60-to-40 ratio of hardscape to landscape.

Photo Details >>>

1: Trellises, a plant bed, and a welcoming bench define the outer edges of the property.
2: A new address marker and entry lantern warm up and personalize the space.
3: Brown concrete pavers represent earth, adding texture to previously flat surfaces.
4: A trellis breaks up the bare expanse of a neighboring wall, adding greenery and texture.

Whether or not you become a feng shui follower, take heed of these strategies to turn your off-kilter house into a flow-right refuge.

Before: An overly formal post lantern and door light **After:** A new address marker and lantern warm the entry **Before:** A tiny lot between two other homes	**After:** Trellises and plant beds that define property edges **Before:** No scents-ual plants **After:** The fragrance of lavender and honeysuckle	**Before:** Silly shutters, frilly scalloped trim, and a superfluous balcony **After:** Thick trim on windows and bold dentil molding to define the garage

1 2
3 4

BEFORE

AFTER

HERE'S WHAT THEY DID

When they discovered that the only creatures that enjoyed their front yard were the neighbor's dogs, Karin and Patrick Smyth realized it was time to make a change.

The busy couple knew that overhauling the gently sloping yard while keeping an eye on their young children would be too much to handle. Luckily, *Curb Appeal* designers Brian Upp and Brian Dittmar were prepared to tackle the task.

The Brians created a symmetrical plan that restored order to the overall landscape. Curved retaining walls create a level, inviting lawn and offset the home's right-angle architecture. Mottled gray landscape blocks used for the retaining walls tie the concrete drive and taupe-gray house together, as well as emphasize the brick path's putty-color mortar.

The unruly plants that dominated one side of the front-door awning and most of the lawn were removed and replaced with understated elements. Sparse flower-filled container pots as well as dogwood and Japanese maple line both sides of the walkway, providing touches of color and balance without overpowering the walk's brickwork. Spiraled topiaries in urns on either side of the front door lend the illusion of added height. The plants' complementary colors, varied shapes and textures, and sundry heights of everything from groundcovers to 5-foot saplings create newfound depth and dimension.

As a finishing touch, window boxes further soften the harsh lines of the split-level home, creating an exterior that calls to passersby, "Come on in!"

Photo Details >>>

1: Stately topiaries in black urns frame the new glass-panel, amber-color wood door.

2: Window boxes add texture and soft shapes to the house facade.

3: A retaining wall helps create a level lawn that invites kids to play.

4: Retaining walls curve slightly, giving the lawn terrace a rounded look to complement the split-level's boxy shape.

Take a cue from the solutions that allowed the Smyths to trade their crazy jungle for a serene Eden.

Before: Old plantings obscuring the brick path and steps **After:** Dogwoods and Japanese maples on either side of the walk	of varied colors, shapes, textures, and plant heights	clashes with the bricks **After:** A new amber-color wood door
Before: One mass of similar-looking plants **After:** An assortment	**Before:** Sloped terrain **After:** Curved retaining walls built from mottled gray landscape blocks **Before:** A red door that	**Before:** An over-whelming expanse of backyard fence **After:** A flowering potato vine climbing the fence adds texture

8

FINISH WITH DETAILS

Dress Your Dwelling in Address Markers, Mailboxes, Lighting, and More

Men have their watches, their ties, their cuff links. Women have handbags, heels, and jewelry. And how does a home polish off its look? With address markers, mailboxes, water fountains, outdoor lanterns, and other finishing touches that make a house either fashionably of-the-moment, a timeless classic, or a funky standout. Adding such trimmings is the least permanent—and typically least expensive—of the makeover options tackled on *Curb Appeal*, and such a low level of commitment carries a whole lot of freedom. Feel like stenciling flowers on your mailbox? Have at it. Envision an oar blade as your address marker? Paddle on. Dream of twinkling garden lights? Plug it in. The beauty in dressing up your front yard with such particulars is that changing them out is just as easy as setting them up. To complete your home's transformation, browse on to learn the best ways to add oomph and overall curb appeal.

Analyze to Accessorize

Adding the trimmings doesn't come at the end of a *Curb Appeal* makeover by happenstance. It makes the most sense—after all, you pick your shoes only after you've decided what to wear, right? So take another walk out to the curb to survey the scene.

Ask yourself which existing details work and which don't. During the day, can you clearly spot the address marker? Is the mailbox in good condition? At night, turn on the outdoor lights. Can you easily find the front door and address? Are paths properly lit? Analyze the trappings with functionality and style in mind, then make a list of what's staying and what's needed to fill in the blanks.

Do It Yourself or Hire a Pro? This chapter is do-it-yourself central, but there are a few tasks that are still pro territory. Here's how to know what's in your realm or on their turf:

If you can glue a broken dish together ... Then you can make a bird spa.

If you have a drill and follow directions well ... Then you can change out exterior lighting.

If you string holiday lights on a tree or house ... Then you can install low-voltage garden lights.

If you can plug in an appliance and fill a pitcher of water ... Then you can assemble a water sculpture kit.

If you can hang a picture ... Then you can mount a wall fountain.

If you want to install standard (120 volts) lighting or a complex nightscape ... Then hire a licensed electrician to properly set up the transformer, bury the wires, and conceal the fixtures.

If your fountain is too large for one person to move ... Then have it delivered and hire a contractor to place and install it.

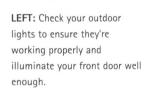

LEFT: Check your outdoor lights to ensure they're working properly and illuminate your front door well enough.

CURB APPEAL COMMENT: Cheat a Little

If cost prohibits you from taking on major changes covered in earlier chapters, feel free to jump ahead and add trimming details. Comply with your overall design plan to maintain your goals and style.

Get Happy With Hardware

Whether you're looking to finish an eye-catching new door or zest up a dull keeper, hardware does the trick every time. This mini-facelift has major impact on one of the most prominent features of the house.

Because door hardware is important to your home's overall look, don't rush to pick the first doorknob or handle, hinges, kick plate, and door knocker you see. Instead, use these tips to land on the right equipment.

> **Follow the door's lead.** If it sports metal detailing or wears leaded glass, match metals or paint the hardware black.

> **Be period correct.** Choose vintage or reproduction hardware that keeps with your house style.

> **Let architectural details dictate** hardware choices. For instance, if you have black wrought ironwork on the front of your house, consider dark or iron hand-hewn handles or knobs and plates. If your house has a cottage or Tudor style and a large wood door, opt for pronounced decorative hinges. For a modern home with a painted metal door, look for stainless-steel hardware.

> **Keep weathering in mind.** If you are in an area exposed to weathering agents such as wet, salty air, choose hardware that can resist them.

> **Use the same (or a similar) hardware style** on your garage as you do on your front door.

THIS PAGE: Hardware is available in a plethora of styles, shapes, and finishes. Choose pieces that complement the rest of your home's exterior.

OPPOSITE: Craftsman-style details in the door hardware, lights, and accessories enhance the architecture of this home.

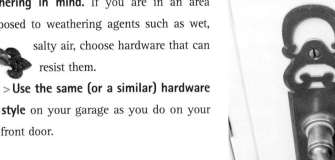

HOUSE RENDER REMINDER

If you add large-scale trimmings, add them to your house rendering and site plan, and your sketches are complete. Frame each or place them in a keepsake before-and-after makeover brag book. Once your yard grows in, take another "after" photo for the cover.

Add Awesome Address Markers

Address markers are essential for receiving that birthday package from Mom, getting the delivery pizza while the big game's still on, and helping guests arrive on time. Obviously visibility and legibility are musts.

From the curbside, determine where to place numbers. On a street side fence post? Near the front door? On the garage? Pick a number size large enough to read from a passing car. From there, style takes over. Browsing local hardware and home improvement centers for ideas, you'll find an array of metal and ceramic options. Past *Curb Appeal* episodes pepped up the standards: Homeowners covered generic versions with copper sheeting; suspended numerals on a stone for a mini-sculpture; and placed number stickers on an oar face. Follow suit and stroll off the beaten path for markers that both stand out and mesh perfectly with your home's new design scheme.

Shop Smart

Look for address numbers, mailbox options, and yard art at local craft, hobby, home, and garden shops. If they don't yield what you need, surf online or order custom fare.

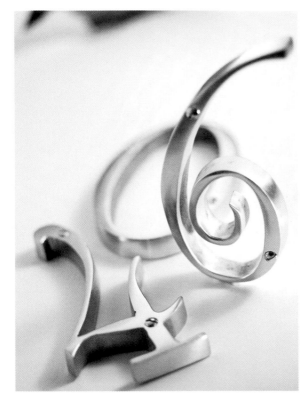

CURB APPEAL

COMMENT: Metal Mania

Cover generic house address numbers with copper sheeting for a timeless look.

Make Your Mailbox Marvelous

A mailbox is more than a vessel for the bills you would rather not receive and the packages you can't wait to open. Regardless of where you place your mailbox, make sure it conveys your home's personality to the letter carrier and all who pass by.

BELOW: Whether you choose a posted or hanging mailbox, make sure it melds with your home's style.

OPPOSITE: A structured box such as this one is not only sturdy, it also emulates the shape of the gate behind it.

Just remember to abide by Uncle Sam and do your hometown homework before choosing from these three basic types.

> **Posted box.** Posted mailboxes typically suffer from a bad case of afterthought, which is pretty criminal when you've just given your home a major facelift. Rather than sticking a government-issued box on an unpainted 2×2 and plunking it down by the curb, exert a little more effort for style's sake. At the very least, stain or paint wooden posts to suit a house's trim and woodwork. Or go beyond the basic and get a little artsy. Spell out house numbers in mosaic tiles glued on the siding or door. Stencil on a design inspired by your house—perhaps grapes and vines for a Tuscan villa? If space permits, plant a small bed of flowers or a tame groundcover around the base.

> **Structured box.** Setting your box in a substantial structure protects it from cars and vandals. And since designing and building such a thing is no small-scale affair, enlist a pro to create and install one that complements your house and front yard. Echo materials used elsewhere in your hardscape, such as bricks, stones, and masonry, and soften the look with side beds or a blooming vine trained up the base. In some cases you might even use a sculpture to encase the mailbox.

> **Hanging drop box.** Hanging boxes include everything from cheery-red metal models that bear gold horns and crowns, to sweetly painted ceramic demi-pots, to brushed-steel files that reek of efficiency. Take your cue from your house trimmings (hinges, ironwork, the front door, and doorbell) and pick a hanging box in keeping with those materials and looks. Ceramics look great with stucco houses, stainless-steel finishes complete modernized ranches, and bright-color, glossy paints look smart on any white home.

Love Your Lighting

"Leave the light on" is the age-old way to welcome loved ones home. Beyond being a cozy come-hither, good lighting guides the way to your front door or garage; boosts safety; increases security; and adds ambience to any garden.

As you devise the best lighting plan for your front yard, keep these tips in mind.

Tip One: Match the style of house-mounted fixtures to your home's architecture: hand-hewn designs with earthy cottages; modern looks with cool cottages and streamlined ranches; and elegant and classic silhouettes with stately manors, for example.

Tip Two: Use similar light fixtures for the front door, porch, and garage.

Tip Three: Replace any industrial-looking bare-bulb spotlights with encased, stylized lanterns or recessed lights.

Tip Four: Rather than the stark security lights of the past, buy mount plates with embedded motion sensors or opt for lanterns with built-in sensors.

Tip Five: Install garden lights after the landscaping is complete.

Tip Seven: Install battery-powered outdoor lighting on paths if wiring isn't feasible.

Tip Eight: Use light-sensing or solar-powered garden lights to save money.

Tip Nine: Camouflage accent garden lighting by placing fixtures in discreet spots.

Tip Ten: Test-drive garden lights at night to perfect their locations.

Tip Eleven: Use green (or verdigris) garden lanterns to blend fixtures into a landscape.

Tip Twelve: Move lights that highlight garden features to showcase the current season's best elements.

Garden Light, Garden Bright

The sun may have set, but your new front yard hasn't lost any of its charm. Install landscape lighting to showcase the landscape at night and recover a total return on your makeover investment. Play up the most striking elements (significant trees, water fountains, sculptures) with these three basic lighting techniques—or even better, a combination of them all:

Uplighting: Placed below an object, lights shine directly upward and cast shadows behind the figure.

Downlighting: Lights mounted above an object, illuminating it like moonlight or sunshine.

Sidelighting: Lights set beside an object, highlighting swaths and portions of it.

Tip Six: Choose the proper voltage for garden lights. Low-voltage varieties (12 volts) are typically strung together on spikes and plug into exterior outlets. Standard voltage lights (120 volts) cover a larger territory and put out more light, but involve submerged wiring and require a licensed electrician to install in accordance with local codes.

CURB APPEAL COMMENT: Hide It Away

Secure all outdoor light and pump electrical cords and camouflage them with paint that blends into the surroundings.

Adore Your Art

A fully made over front yard and house create an ideal backdrop for outdoor art. And since even the most traditionally landscaped and painted house could use a little public display of your private personality, why not finish off the decorating job with a must-have piece?

Build a Bird Spa

For less than $25 and in less than an hour, you can build a super-basic, super-sturdy, bird-friendly spa. Place seeds in the top and it's a feeder; pour in a little water and it's a bath.

Step One: Gather two to three terra-cotta pots in ascending sizes.

Step Two: Flip pots over and stack them atop each other, mouth over bottom, to form the spa base. Add a third pot if extra height is needed.

Step Three: Buy or recycle a saucer (to scale) to sit atop the base. Terra-cotta pot dishes or sturdy, shallow ceramic bowls work well. If used as a feeder, coat the dish with nontoxic glaze to protect birds.

Step Four: Attach the saucer top to the base with weatherproof garden glue.

Step Five: Paint the pots to suit your landscape and house or leave them natural.

Step Six: Place the spa; fill tray with water or seeds.

THIS PAGE: Choose accessories that suit your style and enhance the exterior of your home.

Search local garden centers, antique malls, salvage depots, crafts shops, statuary stores, and arts festivals for finds. Then place your treasure as a prominent greeter (in the middle of a courtyard) or as a surprise side note (tucked away in a flower bed). Situate a piece as you would a container pot—on level ground so it's visible both coming and going—or near benches and other sitting areas. Choose art in harmony with your landscape's natural palette: greens and browns in woodland settings; bright rainbow shades in flower gardens. Keep in step with exterior elements. Place copper or metal sculptures near copper-top fences; a worn stone statue near a weathered stone wall.

Once you become an outdoor art aficionado, don't overwhelm your space with a slew of knick-knacks; rather, choose pieces of substance and rotate them throughout the year. Here are some best-in-show choices.

- Birdbath, feeder, and spa
- Gazing balls
- Metal cutouts
- Sculptures
- Statuary
- Sundials
- Tromp l'oeil wall murals
- Weather vanes
- Wind chimes

CURB APPEAL COMMENT: Use Your Walls

Walls under the eaves of the house are ideal for displaying art outdoors. They provide semiprotected backdrops for weather-resistant pieces—particularly those constructed from materials such as clay, wire, and redwood.

Flip Over Fountains

Aside from yard art, few things capture your attention like a water sculpture: The burbling sounds soothe and make hot days feel cooler by suggestion alone. If you're feeling crafty, set aside one-half hour one afternoon and create a water sculpture of your own.

OPPOSITE: Fountains require periodic maintenance to look their best. At a minimum, refill as needed to keep water levels consistent and remove debris regularly.

Because fountains come in small (wall-mounted), medium (container-pot bound), and large (freestanding cascades), there are options for every budget and space. As with other trimmings, choose materials such as stone, concrete, ceramic, and metal that make sense with your setting. Beyond that, place fountains on level ground in optimum hearing and sight vantage points; avoid spots in leaf-dropping range, as debris clogs pumps; and if you have children, place fountains out of toddlers' reach.

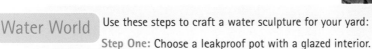 Water World   Use these steps to craft a water sculpture for your yard:

Step One: Choose a leakproof pot with a glazed interior.

Step Two: Buy a bamboo pump kit, with a shelf that can sit across the mouth of your container.

Step Three: Set the pump at the bottom of the pot, placed against one side.

Step Four: Connect the hose to the pump, then use rocks, gravel, stones, or a brick to secure the pump in place.

Step Five: Attach the free end of the hose to the back end of the spigot, and lay the bamboo shelf across the pot opening, cheating it to one side.

Step Six: Put the fountain in an ideal spot, and fill it with water, plug it in, and turn it on.

BEFORE

AFTER

HERE'S WHAT THEY DID

The Malatestas are a funky bunch, with an eclectic menagerie under one roof: One daughter owns a gecko; another cares for a corn snake; and Bella, the chocolate Lab, wanders where she pleases. Given this laid-back love of the offbeat, the family's house came off as more stoic than any of its residents, and everyone was ready for a sassed-up change. *Curb Appeal* designer Mark Pellegrino jumped at the chance to dress the place in a way that celebrated the family's quirky interests and their love of the outdoors.

In shaking off the Southern colonial's straight-lace style, Mark chose to focus on the details. He replaced the outdated transom with a neutral, elegant one detailed with hand-etched magnolias. The same detailing is present on the new black metal mailbox.

Before, the address markers over the front door were so large they detracted from the rest of the house. Now, simple brass address numerals above the garage are visible without drawing attention from the rest of the house. Once visitors reach the front door, they are greeted by a new gecko-shape doorbell plate, which offers a clue as to what they'll find inside.

To create a space for the family to relax outdoors, Mark covered the old concrete porch floor with slate flagstone and added a coir welcome mat. A cozy bench tucked between two spacious windows and new garden lights provide an outdoor space for the Malatestas to convene even after dark. To complete the scene, a bubbling fountain adds the soothing sound of water.

Photo Details >>>

1: A bubbling water fountain surrounded by swaying grasses adds a classic Southern element.
2: In an homage to the household reptile lovers, the new doorbell plate is shaped like a gecko.
3: Slate flagstone flooring covers the previously cold concrete floor.
4: The new fixtures, door hardware, pots, and freshly painted shutters complement the home's brick facade.

Whether finishing touches are the last step of your makeover or all your house needs, try some of the tricks that branded the Malatestas' home as their own.

Before: No front-yard focal point
After: A bubbling water fountain

Before: No place to sit on the expansive porch
After: A cozy, family-size bench

Before: Oversize address markers over the front door
After: Smaller brass address numerals set over the garage

Before: Poor nighttime lighting
After: New garden lights and lanterns

Before: No rugs to stop mud at the front door
After: A earthy coir welcome mat

1 2
3 4

9

DO THE HOMEWORK

Hire Cream-of-the-Crop Crews, Dodge Disasters, and Learn the Law

Most *Curb Appeal* episodes come off without a hitch. Sure, designers and homeowners may haggle a little over paint colors; landscaping plans might weather a bit of tweaking; and budgets have scaled back a dream or two. But that's par for the course with any collaborative effort. What you don't see each week are run-ins with local neighborhood associations, sites shutting down thanks to code violations, or area evacuations due to gas leaks. Why the lack of such construction drama? Because *Curb Appeal* homeowners—and the crews that help them realize their dreams—do their homework. That's what this chapter is all about: tending to issues before they become problems. If you want to spare yourself unnecessary trouble and expense, school yourself with the following pages before you pick up the phone for that first project bid.

Know Your Crew

Knowing who does what on a makeover crew prevents the ever-annoying and pricey expense of you having to tackle someone else's job at the last minute or, even worse, hiring two people to do the same thing.

Study this cast of characters. They are the ones who likely will bring your outdoor makeover to life.

> **Architect.** A licensed professional who designs buildings of all scales. Because many architects tend toward commercial and large public properties, look for someone who specializes in residential construction. Hire an architect if you are making major structural changes to your house facade and see that he or she is certified as a Registered Architect (RA).

> **Building Designer.** Like architects, designers also draw up plans for buildings, but unlike architects, they are not fully licensed. Those accredited with Certified Professional Building Designer (CPBD) degrees have spent years practicing in the field and have passed intense certification testing to attain this level. Note that as a rule, designers charge up to about 6 percent less than architects, and you may never know the difference in deliverables.

> **Landscape Architect.** A state-licensed professional who does land planning and designs outdoor spaces, structures, and hardscapes. Most landscape architects tend toward large-scale public and commercial projects. Look for professionals who excel in residential work, and are registered by the American Society of Landscape Architects (ASLA), a highly selective professional organization.

Hire a Dream Makeover Team

Pick the best makeover team to suit your needs and style by following these Dos:

Do ask friends and neighbors whom they recommend and about their experiences with them.

Do check out references before hiring anyone.

Do inquire about candidates' timelines of past projects as well as work quality.

Do look for complaints filed with the local Better Business Bureau.

Do visit past projects overseen by potential architects, designers, and contractors.

Do request itemized estimates.

Do inquire about materials—sources and specifics—to ensure quality. For example, what type of wood is to be used and what supplier would it come from?

LEFT: Choosing an architect or designer who understands what you wish to do is pivotal for a successful project.

OPPOSITE: A landscape designer or architect will envision your green spaces; an architect or building designer can handle the structural details.

> **Landscape designer.** Unlicensed designers whose work and expertise vary by experience, landscape designers often handle residential projects. They can be as well-versed as a landscape architect yet cost less, and some even know plant lists better than their licensed counterparts. Look for individuals registered by the Association of Professional Landscape Designers (APLD).

> **Garden designer.** Unlicensed specialists who typically focus on small, theme-based gardens (such as water gardens, cottage gardens, or formal labyrinths) rather than large yards. Their experience and expertise vary from person to person.

> **Contractor.** Certified and bonded professionals who oversee crews and/or perform the work needed to transform building and landscape designs into reality. Locally licensed to perform work and run a business, they have the authority and experience to obtain the necessary permits required for landscape and construction work.

> **Subcontractor.** A bonded specialist hired by a contractor to complete a particular project, such as masonry, painting, or fence-building.

ABOVE: An architect or building designer can help integrate a new portico into the existing rooflines and ensure the addition looks proportional to the house.

OPPOSITE LEFT: Replacing existing steps probably only requires a contractor who specializes in concrete. To completely rework an entry, consult with an architect or building designer.

OPPOSITE RIGHT: On *Curb Appeal*, professionals are available from the beginning. During your remodel, consult with the pros early on to determine how they might help.

Obey the Law

Unless you're doing no more than adding a container pot to your front stoop, you're best served diving into the legalities of home makeovers. A little local research could save you from expensive fines tomorrow.

Keep these Dos in mind to ensure every move you make with your personal curb appeal project is on the up-and-up.

- **Do** secure building and landscaping permits.
- **Do** post permits as required.
- **Do** learn the meaning of codes, easements, deed, variances, and more. (See the glossary on page 188.)
- **Do** learn any deed restrictions that dictate what you can and can't do on your property.
- **Do** go to your local town hall and architectural review boards to research regulations that govern building and landscaping projects. Or rely on the expertise of your contractor and design professionals.
- **Do** check with your neighborhood association to learn residential project restrictions.
- **Do** share neighborhood restrictions with contractors and design professionals.

RIGHT: Before you begin building, ensure that your plans adhere to local regulations and neighborhood association restrictions.

OPPOSITE: Check with local agencies about possible restrictions regarding building decks and railings.

CURB APPEAL COMMENT: avoid the Wall of Shame

Just about every town has building codes stating just how high a fence or wall can be—or evenif you can have a fence around your front yard. Save yourself a major redo by making sure you know the restrictions before you build.

It's the Law

Local agencies and neighborhood associations can regulate everything from the types of plants you install, to the color you paint your house, to where you place a patio. Look up restrictions in your area if you are adding any of the following:

- Balconies
- Decks
- Fences and walls
- Outbuilding construction
- Public plantings (the sidewalk area)
- Railings
- Ramps
- Steps
- Water structures

Learn the Key Terms

Learning the language of the experts is the first step toward understanding what they're saying. Whether you're double-checking local codes or signing legal documents with your contractor, a grasp of building concepts goes a long way.

OPPOSITE: Before adding a porch to the front of your home, check local codes. You'll likely need a permit and approved plans. Your plans may need to compensate for setback regulations if your home sits close to property lines.

RIGHT: In most neighborhoods even something as seemingly simple as a walkway needs to comply with codes.

Familiarize yourself with these common terms vital to the legalities of home and yard improvement projects.

> **Bonded.** Insurance policies contractors get to protect their business against bankruptcy in lieu of a suit. Protects both hired and hiring parties.

> **Code.** Government regulations that specify construction parameters. Can include landscape, structural, or cosmetic changes.

> **Deed.** A document certifying the transfer of property. May contain built-in restrictions of what can and cannot be built on a lot or house.

> **Easement.** The right to use someone else's property for a specified purpose. For example, your local government may run a sewage line through your property because of an easement on your lot. Don't build or erect garden structures on land covered by an easement.

> **Frontage.** The borderline of a property that fronts another element, such as a street, a ditch, or a sidewalk. Neighborhood associations and other governing bodies might regulate street frontage plantings and construction of things such as mailboxes.

> **Permit.** Permission from local government that allows construction, maintenance, or landscaping work to be performed. Can be obtained by contractors, builders, or property owners who meet locally specified requirements.

> **Right of Way.** Land that includes an easement for others to move across a part of your property. A right of way might be the green space between your curb and the street, which is public domain but privately maintained.

> **Setback.** The distance a structure must stand away from a property line.

> **Title.** Proof of property ownership.

> **Variance.** Permission from a local zoning board to stray from code governing home and lot improvements.

CURB APPEAL COMMENT: Weigh In

Bay windows and balconies are fabulous for home fronts. But they add weight to the front of your house. Be sure your walls can handle the extra load.

Set Up a Safe and Sound Construction Site

Before you break ground, tend to basic construction site details to avoid disasters such as gushing water mains and collapsing staircases. The time you spend now focusing on the details will save you tons of time and money down the road.

Use the ideas on this checklist to ensure you've got all the bases covered before construction begins.

- Call the power, gas, electric, cable, and water companies to learn the location of underground lines and pipes before you start digging.
- Ensure that columns are not load-bearing before you tear them down.
- Wear protective gear while tearing down walls, columns, and fences and ripping up concrete.
- Have major structural and landscape work designed, built, installed, and removed by pros.
- Get the proper instruction before using major equipment, especially jackhammers, backhoes, and other rental equipment.
- Hire pros to remove large trees, fences, and other structures, including power lines.
- Check that you have the proper voltage capabilities before installing outdoor lighting. When in doubt, consult with a licensed electrician.

RIGHT: Before the heavy equipment rolls in, review renovation plans with all involved parties and have utility companies mark the location of underground lines and pipes.

- Use weatherproof extension cords for exposed lighting and water features. Do-it-yourselfers can tackle aboveground wiring, but contractors should install belowground conduits.
- Build additions in front of existing water spigots and dryer vents only after you've rerouted pipe flow.
- Turn off all outdoor light breakers before replacing exterior fixtures.

CURB APPEAL COMMENT: Get a Grip on Drips

When one *Curb Appeal* homeowner decided to yank a front stair off his house, the falling structure knocked off an exterior spigot. Fortunately, the homeowner knew how to turn off the spewing water and had planned to shut it off to make way for new construction.

Create a Set-in-Stone Contract

Get project details ironed out in a written, legal contract to protect all parties in case something goes awry.

Do familiarize yourself with sample home and yard construction contracts before entering negotiations. Search online and software sources for such documents.

Do include a timeline with specific start and end dates.

Do determine that all contractors and workers are covered by liability and property insurance and are bonded too.

Do look into fixed-term contracts, which stipulate that payments depend on finish dates.

Do put payment plans into the contract. Deliver the last installment only when all work is completed.

Do have all relevant parties initial and date any contract changes.

Be Nice to Your Neighbors

Your home may be your castle, but there's no getting around getting along with the neighboring kingdoms. Run plans that may impact your neighbors by them early on so you can all live happily ever after.

THIS PAGE: Curbside plantings and fences may increase the curb appeal of your own home, but also consider how your choices will impact neighbors' yards.

OPPOSITE: A multilevel terrace serves as a welcoming entrance point to a charming cottage. The homeowners considered the views of the neighborhood from the terrace, as well as how the new addition would look from their neighbors' homes across the street.

An important aspect of curb appeal is that it appeals to your neighbors and other passersby. After all, depending on their location they may have the opportunity to see the exterior of your home more than you do. While you probably don't need to get your neighbors' approval for your plans—unless a neighborhood convenant requires it—you do want to consider your project from their point of view.

Heed this diplomatic advice to sidestep touchy makeover problems.

- **Do** learn your true property lines as noted on your property title or deed.
- **Do** inform neighbors of pending work and plans.
- **Do** erect new fences and walls on setbacks rather than on property lines.
- **Do** compromise if you share the same property-marking wall or fence and want to renovate it.
- **Do** avoid creating drainage, vine, leaf-, or fruit-dropping issues for neighbors.
- **Do** check that fences and walls are attractive from your side and your neighbor's.

- **Do** borrow neighbors' good views and tastefully screen out unfavorable views.
- **Do** speak tactfully: Tell neighbors you are boosting your own privacy, not blocking out views of their not-so-pretty property.

 **COMMENT: Color Me Glad**

Urban makeovers mean working within your neighbors' general color palette, thanks to proximity. Whenever Curb Appeal does a makeover, the designers make sure the final color fits both the house style and the neighborhood.

Secure Your Home

Some locations—and homeowners—demand a heightened level of security for their homes. Whether you're designing a new landscape or installing surveillance equipment, consider your home's security as you begin your project.

THIS PAGE: Home security may be as simple as installing deadbolts or as high-tech as an alarm system.

OPPOSITE: Strategically placed plantings may deter intruders, but be sure to install secure doors and windows as well.

Safety shouldn't be an unattractive afterthought to your exterior makeover. Many exterior safety measures can actually increase curb appeal. Keeping foundation shrubs neatly clipped, for example, minimizes places for an intruder to hide. Pruning low-hanging tree branches near your home spruces up the landscape, and eliminates a would-be route for a prowler. When it comes to safety, keep these Dos in mind:

- **Do** install security-specific doors, walls, and gates as needed.
- **Do** use keypad front-door entries and remote-controlled garage doors.
- **Do** monitor entryways with video cameras.
- **Do** set up night lighting throughout your front, back, and side yards.
- **Do** post motion-sensing lights around the perimeter of your house and property.
- **Do** trim shrubs, trees, and other sizable plantings to cut down on overgrown hiding places.
- **Do** plant plants with thorns, barbs, and prickles near vulnerable areas like windows and gates. Incorporate such plants in property line hedges, too.

 **COMMENT: Secure Yourself**

One urban *Curb Appeal* homeowner had a thing for gadgets and security systems. To protect his wife and their small child, he installed keypads and wireless video cameras at the street gate and house door, which fed info to the home computer system.

1776

BEFORE

AFTER

HERE'S WHAT THEY DID

The weedy "lawn" and withered hydrangea at the bottom of Jennifer Nam and John Reyes' home made it evident: This couple didn't care much for yard care. In fact, the newlywed first-time homeowners were so ashamed of their landscape, they only invited friends over in the evenings, when the lot would be cloaked in darkness. Since that's no way for a spunky pair to start off their life together, *Curb Appeal* home designer Shannon Mitchell and landscape planner Cody Shrey overhauled the old yard to take it from shameful to stunning.

Because it's unlikely that either husband or wife would sprout a green thumb overnight, the design team incorporated an easy-tend landscape that softened the house facade. The first step was to fix the sloping yard by adding a gentle retaining wall to prevent erosion. Then, pruned trees, sod, and hardy plant specimens were added to breathe life into the space. One-season annuals lend low-commitment color to the flower beds, while shrubs and leafy grasses break up the space with their varied hues.

To fix the disjointed exterior color palette and create an uncluttered, harmonious backdrop, the *Curb Appeal* designers stained the concrete drive, added a rich burgundy door, and covered the brick stairs with gray slate. As a finishing touch that shows off the couple's sassy personalities, John used his newfound welding skills to craft a metal cat sculpture placed by the front walk, and Jennifer built an outdoor-safe mosaic table set in the far corner of the yard for socializing.

Photo Details >>>

1: Replacing a bright red door, the new, rich burgundy one blends seamlessly with its surroundings.
2: Stones mimicking a dry creek bed support front walkway stairs.
3: Gray slate covers the brick stairs, providing a subdued transition between the house and yard.
4: A new garage door and stylish house numbers up the driveway's appeal.

For a friendly, low-maintenance update that won't break the bank, check out the following tips.

Before: Overgrown trees and weeds littered the property
After: Pruned trees, new sod, and plant specimens add color

Before: Mismatched elements created a disjointed exterior palette

After: Stained concrete, a new door, and slate-covered bricks make a harmonious backdrop

Before: No transition between the asphalt drive, street, and green space
After: Mulch-covered

beds add curvy silhouettes and texture

Before: No blooms or healthy plants in the monochromatic yard
After: One-season annuals, shrubs, and leafy grasses in varied hues

1 2
3 4

BEFORE

AFTER

HERE'S WHAT THEY DID

When the Websters bought wife Christy's childhood home from her mom, they thought it was the perfect place to raise their own kids, except for one problem.

Although the family adored the split-level's interior, the dated exterior wasn't working for them. So *Curb Appeal* designer Megan Clark and landscape designer Brad Frazier came to the rescue. Their goal? To transform the '70s time capsule into a modern-day marvel with the hints of Craftsman cool that Christy and Warren craved.

This involved ditching the home's drab color palette leftover from the '70s in favor of a combination of earthy taupe, crisp white, and cranberry red.

The crisp white is visible on the thick trim that surrounds the balcony's new glass French doors. It is also evident on the Craftsman-inspired wood railings that anchor the balcony and porch. So the new porch railings aren't hidden by the front yard's overgrown hedges, Clark and Frazier replaced the old shrubs with a combination of shade-loving ferns and hydrangeas.

Revamped doors made a major impact. The front door is cranberry red to draw guests' attention. A new garage door sports windows, paneling, and thick trim for a carriage-house look. Both the garage and front doors are flanked by Craftsman-style lanterns and feature arched windows that add curves to the otherwise straight house facade

Faux stone-covered cement pillars delineate the drive and match the new stones covering the retaining wall bordering the yard. One pillar even pulls double-duty as a mailbox.

Photo Details >>>

1: A red door pops out from the shade and contrasts with the house.
2: A new layer of faux stone set in mortar gives the retaining wall a natural, textured look.
3: Faux stone cement pillars set off the drive's entrance and stylishly house the mailbox.
4: A new garage door, larger lanterns, and solid white wood railings on the balcony are instances of Craftsman style.

Here's how a fresh color scheme, a new front yard, and architectural swap-outs helped the Websters' house grow up.

Before: Hedges hiding the front porch **After:** Lush, low-growing foundation plantings	**Before:** A blah garage door **After:** Windows, paneling, and thick trim in carriage-house style	Craftsman-inspired wood railings
Before: Tiny garage and entry fixtures **After:** Proportional Craftsman-style lanterns	**Before:** Skinny iron railings on the porch and balcony **After:** White-painted,	**Before:** Worn-out shutters and windows on the upper porch **After:** Glass French doors, thick new trim

1 2
3 4

Glossary

A

Acidic soil: Soil with a pH level less than 7.

Address marker: Numbers that state an address.

Annual: Plant that lives a few seasons and dies without regenerating. Usually added to landscapes for colorful blooms and leaves.

Al fresco: Outdoors, in the fresh air.

Alkaline soil: Soil with a pH level greater than 7.

Arbor: Latticed frame over which vines grow. Typically shaped like a doorframe to create an entryway or focal point.

Architect: A licensed professional who designs buildings and structures of all scales.

Awning: A sheltering overhang above a door, window, or seating area. Can be made of canvas or other materials.

B

Backfill: Soil removed from and returned to an area to fill in holes and level slopes.

Berm: A mound of earth adding contour to a terrain.

Boardwalk: A path of wood planks.

Bone structure: The lines and silhouette of an object or space and its defining details.

C

Clad: Covered.

Coir mat: Mat of coconut husk fibers.

Color scheme: Three to four complementary colors chosen from a palette to unify any scene—a house exterior or landscape, for example.

Color palette: A group of harmonious colors from which a color scheme is selected.

Color wheel: A circular diagram charting a full range of colors, arranged so like colors and shades are side-by-side, and complementary colors are across from one another. Tool used to determine coordinating colors in palettes and schemes.

Column: A vertical shaft used to support an overhanging structure or architectural element. Typically consists of a pediment (base) and capital (uppermost capping).

Compost: Decaying organic material that enriches soil to promote plant growth. Ideally comprises both green matter (grass and clippings) and brown matter (dead leaves and branches).

Container: The vessel in which flowers, plants, trees, shrubs, or a combination are planted. Can include pots, planters, windowboxes, and found objects.

Contrast: Design principle that emphasizes the differences between two compared objects, shapes, colors, or textures.

Contractor: Licensed and bonded professional who oversees (and/or performs) the work and crews needed to transform building and landscape designs into reality.

Cornice: In exterior architecture, molding that projects from a wall, topping off an entablature or simply acting as a decorative mantle.

D

Deciduous: Plant that sheds leaves each year before going dormant and hibernating for a season.

Demi-pot: A pot cut in half to create a semi-circle. Placed against or hung upon a wall.

Designer: Unlicensed but experienced architectural and/or landscape professional who creates hardscape and/or landscape plans. Typically specializes in and excels at residential projects.

Detailing: Design element that embellishes an object with unique or ornate character.

Dormer: A vertical window that projects from a sloped roof and typically topped with a gable.

Downspout: A pipe that leads from roof gutters to the ground.

Drip line: Line that marks where cascading water falls or drips down from a tree canopy or roofline.

E

Entablature: In classical architecture, the term for the gable-shaped face of a portico (or similarly decorative molding) supported by columns.

Evergreen: Plant that retains its leaves and color year-round.

Extension agent: County government employee who assists local farmers and gardeners with bettering their crops, soil, and land conditions.

F

Flagstone: A flat slab of stone used in paving hardscapes or as single step-pingstones.

Flora: Plant material.

Focal point: An object that is the center of attention in a space.

Foundation planting: Collection of plants, flowers, trees, and shrubs that encircles a house to conceal the foundation.

French drain: A subterranean drainage tunnel that reroutes water from a soggy location to a dry one.

G

Gable: A triangular wallfront seen on some rooflines; tops some windows (dormers) and doors.

Glazing: The glass of a window.

Glazing compound: Sealant applied to the seams of window elements. Viscous when applied; dries hard.

Groundcover: Material that covers an area of otherwise bare earth. Can be organic (barking, pine straw) or a low plant (typically a short grass or creeping vine).

H

Hardscape: Non-living structures like driveways, paths, walls, fences, courtyards, and buildings in an environment.

Hue: Various shades of the same color.

L

Landing: The platform at the top of a flight of stairs or short series of steps.

Landscape: Overarching term for the terrain, topography, and all living elements in an environment (such as plants and trees).

Landscape architect: A state-licensed professional who sculpts and plans land for development, and designs outdoor spaces, structures, and hardscapes.

Landscape block: Concrete rectangular block used to create walls and structures in an outdoor environment.

Landscape fabric: Permeable material spread over the ground to prevent soil erosion and weeds, or used below ground in French drains. Plants can be planted in holes cut into the fabric so water runoff won't wash away the underlying earth.

Lattice: Crisscrossed strips (typically wood or metal) that form a pierced frame. Can create a trellis, partition panel, or the wall of an outdoor structure such as an arbor.

Latex paint: Water-based paint that dries faster than oil paints. Latex paint spills are more easily cleaned as well.

Leaded glass: Glass (glazing) set in a metal frame to create a window. Can be stained (colored) or clear.

Load-bearing: A structure that supports weight. For example, some columns and walls bear a roof's weight.

Louvers: Flats that cover an open window for ventilation purposes.

M

Millwork: Manufactured detailed woodwork.

Molding: Decorative trim used to frame windows and other architectural details.

Mortar: A bonding material (usually cement) that joins stones or bricks to secure a wall in place.

Muntin: Strip of wood, metal, or synthetics that secures windowpanes together.

O

Oil paint: Paint with an oil base. Works well on irregular surfaces and improves moisture resistance. Is difficult to clean when spilled and has a long drying time.

P

pH: Measurement unit that ranges from 0 to 14 and gauges if soil is acidic or alkaline. Ideal pH level for most plants is 7.0. Soil amendments manipulate pH to reach desired level.

Paint chip strip: A paper strip bearing several related paint color samples. Used to select hues of paint.

Pane: A single portion of a window made of glazing and framed by muntins.

Patina: Adjective that describes the weathered look a material gains with age.

Paver: Concrete block used to create a hardscape surface or edging.

Pediment: A wide, triangular gable used to adorn the top of an entrance or window.

Pergola: A substantial garden structure consisting of columns and overhead beams.

Perrenial: Plant that returns after dormancy for three or more seasons.

Pilaster: Decorative wall feature that appears to be a partial column but is purely ornamental. Often flanks entrances.

Plat: Legal map of a property that outlines permanent structures.

Portico: Overhang with supporting columns attached to a house. Draws attention to an entrance and/or covers a landing or small patio.

Propagate: A plant that multiplies and spreads on its own.

Prune: Periodic cutting back and trimming that allows plants to maintain shape and health.

R

Rendering: A drawing that illustrates a curbside view of a property.

Replacement window: Typically custom-sized window unit that replaces an existing damaged units.

Retaining wall: A wall on a slope that holds earth in place. A terraced hillside includes a series of retaining walls.

Riser: The horizontal portion of a step facing outward, it determines the height (or rise) of each step.

Rootball: A round mix of roots and soil that forms the base of any plant, tree, shrub, or flower.

S

Sash: The outermost part of a window that holds glazing and muntins in place.

Shake: Textured roof or siding tile of wood (or synthetics made to look like wood).

Shingle: Tile of wood, metal, clay, or synthetics used to side and roof houses.

Sidelight: Tall window flanking either side of a door.

Side jamb: Interior window frame panel perpendicular to the sill and sash.

Sod: Turf grass sold in rolled strips to lie atop bare earth for an instant lawn.

Standard voltage lighting: Garden lighting with 120 volts, a transformer, and submerged wiring that requires professional installation.

Stoop: A platform or landing at the top of a series of stairs that leads to a door.

Storm window and door: A secondary window layer added to insulate and protect old, single-pane windows, or a glass version of a screen door seen on older homes. Modern models incorporate all-weatherproofing and energy-efficient qualities into single-unit windows or doors.

Stucco: Plaster used to cover a wall and create a textured, earthy look.

Subcontractor: A bonded specialist hired by contractors to complete a particular project.

Swatch: A portion of a whole.

Swath: A stretch or strip of a surface.

T

Tamp: To press down upon a surface to secure it in place.

Tear sheet: A keepsake sheet of paper torn from a magazine or book.

Terrain: A plot of land and its inherent characteristics.

Terrace: A level stretch of land on a hillside, usually formed with retaining walls. Like the tread on a step.

Till: To loosen and mix up earth in preparation for planting.

Topiary: A plant trained to grow into a specific shape, such as a ball, square, letter, or animal.

Topography: The shape and features of a terrain.

Transom: A window set above a door.

Transformer: An electrical box used to convert the power flow between an outlet and a conduit (or wire) to a compatible voltage level. Used in standard 120-volt garden lighting; requires professional installation.

Tread: The horizontal portion of a step that one lands upon.

Trellis: A latticed structure upon which plants are trained to climb up and grow across.

Trim: Decorative detailing that frames windows, doors, and rooflines. Calls attention to architectural features and adds visual interest.

Trompe l'oiel: French term meaning "fool the eye." Refers to a mural that creates a false scene of true-life proportions.

Turf: Type of grass used to form lawns.

U

Universal: Term that describes the accessibility of doors, entryways, and other spaces. Universal features include ramps, railings, and doors wide enough for a wheelchair to traverse.

V

Verdigris: A green layer of corrosion that forms on untreated, aged copper, brass, and bronze.

Voltage: A measurement of electrical force and power.

W

Window kit: A complete window unit that includes a window frame. Inserted into newly cut openings, or used to replace entire windows and frames.

Window film: An adhesive layer attached to window glazing to improve its energy efficiency.

X

Xeriscape: Dry-clime landscaping that uses drought-resistant and native plants to conserve water.

Z

Zone: A designation that separates the United States into 10 different climates based on temperature. Plants descriptions include zone assignments to ensure hardiness.

Resources

pages 182–183: Webster House

Designers: Megan Clark, Megan Clark of Color; 415/310-5475; megancolor@yahoo.com

Brad Frazier, Landscape Designer, Gardener Brad LLC; 415/846-6291; brad@gardener-brad.com

Cultured Stone: Owens Corning Cultured Stone; 707/422-5871; www.culturedstone.com

Garage Door: Amarr Garage Doors; 336/251-1219; www.amarr.com

Front Doors and French Doors: Simpson Doors; 360/495-3291; www.simpsondoor.com

Exclusively Doors; 415/897-0088

Door Hardware: Doublehill; 714/630-5588; www.simpsondoor.com

Deltana Architectural Hardware; www.deltana.net

Light Fixtures: Bellacor Lights; 877/723-5522; www.bellacor.com

Fabric: Calico Corners; 800/213-6366; www.calicocorners.com

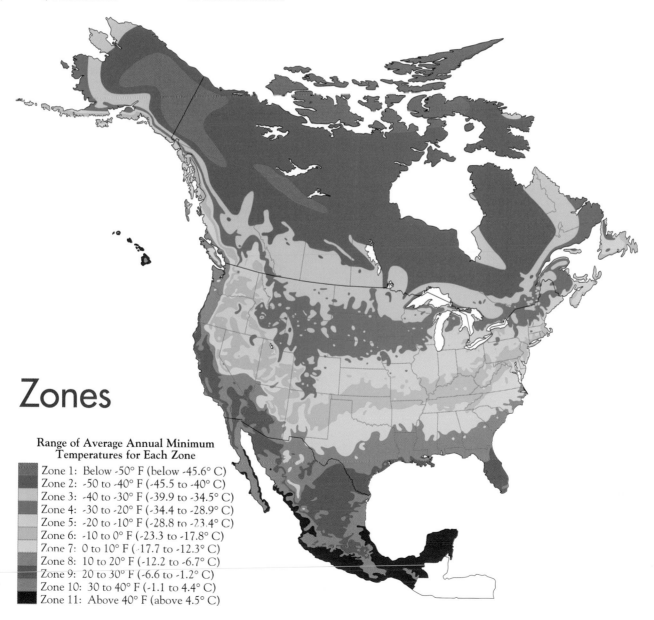

Zones

Range of Average Annual Minimum Temperatures for Each Zone

Zone 1: Below -50° F (below -45.6° C)
Zone 2: -50 to -40° F (-45.5 to -40° C)
Zone 3: -40 to -30° F (-39.9 to -34.5° C)
Zone 4: -30 to -20° F (-34.4 to -28.9° C)
Zone 5: -20 to -10° F (-28.8 to -23.4° C)
Zone 6: -10 to 0° F (-23.3 to -17.8° C)
Zone 7: 0 to 10° F (-17.7 to -12.3° C)
Zone 8: 10 to 20° F (-12.2 to -6.7° C)
Zone 9: 20 to 30° F (-6.6 to -1.2° C)
Zone 10: 30 to 40° F (-1.1 to 4.4° C)
Zone 11: Above 40° F (above 4.5° C)

Index

to some, inspiration comes naturally.
for the rest of us, may we suggest a good book?

Make that three good books. In all three, you'll find simple and affordable design ideas, not to mention plenty of inspiration from HGTV's expert designers.

YOU SHOULD SEE WHAT'S ON HGTV!

HGTV.com